THE PERFECT MILITIA

The Stuart Trained Bands of England and Wales
1603–1642

Peter Leadbetter

'This is the Century of the Soldier', Fulvio Testi, Poet, 1641

Helion & Company

Helion & Company Limited
Unit 8 Amherst Business Centre
Budbrooke Road
Warwick
CV34 5WE
England
Tel. 01926 499 619
Email: info@helion.co.uk
Website: www.helion.co.uk
Twitter: @helionbooks
Visit our blog http://blog.helion.co.uk/

Published by Helion & Company 2021
Designed and typeset by Serena Jones
Cover designed by Paul Hewitt, Battlefield Design (www.battlefield-design.co.uk)

Text © Peter Leadbetter 2021
Illustrations drawn by Alan Turton © Helion & Company 2021
Maps drawn by Derek Tate © 2021
Other images © as individually credited

ISBN 978-1-914059-72-8

British Library Cataloguing-in-Publication Data.
A catalogue record for this book is available from the British Library.

For details of other military history titles published by Helion & Company
Limited, contact the above address, or visit our website: http://www.helion.co.uk

We always welcome receiving book proposals from prospective authors.

Contents

Introduction

Writing this book is probably one of the hardest things I have ever done but it is also probably one of the best things I have ever done. Some readers may disagree with that last comment but, each to their own. The subject of this book, the trained bands in the first half of the seventeenth century, was an organisation that few have ever heard of but they were, in their time, very important within this country and in those days most, if not everyone, knew of them and probably had an opinion of them. There is very little published information on the trained bands so if this book fills some gaps then it has all been worthwhile.

One of the best parts of my research was the travel. I visited most of the county record offices that had documents of interest and a number of libraries, the British Library, the National Library of Wales, the Bodleian Library and the William Salt Library. I also visited Chatsworth House and the National Archives, two very different establishments. I was also able to obtain a number of documents from The Huntington Library in California and the Shakespeare Folger Library in Washington DC although travelling to those two establishments, sadly, was not an option. I would like to thank all those people who were so willing to help me, in person, on the telephone and online.

I am now working on the individual county trained bands which will contain details that were superfluous for this book.

This work has taken over four years and I have to thank my wife Jo for her patience and Derek Tate for the work done on the maps for this book and other maps for my other works. On the subject of maps, I would also like to thank the Cambridge Group, the ESRC, the Leverhulme Trust and the British Academy for permission to use their mapping software.

Any mistakes that anyone finds I will accept responsibility for, and please note that I have expressed some opinions which some readers might not agree with but they are only opinions.

To my knowledge there is no single book currently available that covers the trained bands for the period 1603 to 1642. There is at least one excellent book on the Elizabethan era, *The Elizabethan Militia, 1558–1638*, by Lindsay Boynton published in 1967, which despite the title does contain a chapter each for the reigns of James I and Charles I. Other books and papers are available which cover local government and contain general information on the county trained bands, and a number of books and papers are available on various aspects of the London trained bands. A number of papers also exist for a few of the county trained bands on specific topics but nothing covering the whole organisation, their training or the effectiveness of them.

As far as possible I have used only original documents, this has meant visiting many of the county record offices in England and Wales, looking for relevant material. Other documents have come from the Bodleian Library in Oxford, the National Library of Wales, the National Archives at Kew, the Huntington Library in California, the Folger Shakespeare Library in Washington DC, the British Library and a number of private collections have also been used. I have followed this route because I wanted to make up my own mind using contemporary sources and not use other people's interpretations of that material. This has also meant that if challenged on a point I have the original documentation to back up what I have written. A few transcripts of the county muster books and the deputy lieutenants' letter books are available in print and I have used these whenever possible and also other printed transcripts of relevant documents. These other documents include the constables' accounts and the churchwardens' accounts of towns and villages around the country, both extremely useful sources for low-level military matters.

Give y^r Rest to y^r Musket

2

Sinke downe your right hand not bowing yor body, then gripe your musket and lift it up then bring about the left hand with the rest and joyne it to your Musket, on y^e out side holding yor thumb hard against the forke of the rest and carry both Musket and rest in the left hand only

Author's Note: Drill Manuals

Below is a short introduction to the illustrations penned by Alan Turton, to explain how drill manuals were used by the Trained Bands.

Drill manuals came in two varieties, printed and handwritten. Jenner's *Military Discipline* (as illustrated herein by Alan Turton) is an example of a printed manual. Thomas Jenner was only the publisher of this manual, which was published in 1642; the captions appear to have been copied from Jacob de Gheyn's manual which was issued by the Privy Council for use in the county musters in 1631, with only the spelling of a few words changed. De Gheyn's 1631 manual was an updated edition of his 1607 training manual.

The illustrations used in Jacob de Gheyn's manual were mostly of the same style of dress, unlike those used by Thomas Jenner. A quick look through those included here from Jenner's manual show musketeers dressed very differently; for example, figures 11 and 14 are wearing cavalry boots complete with spurs. The headdress of the musketeers also varies, with a number of different styles illustrated. This lack of uniformity seems to indicate that these were not members of the London Trained Bands but gentlemen from the Artillery Gardens.

So how were the manuals used? The thought in London was that if manuals were sent to the counties then the deputy lieutenants and the officers in the trained bands would read them and improve their military knowledge. Some of the manuals included details of how companies should be organised, and basic advice on battlefield tactics. Needless to say, these manuals were not always read. In Northamptonshire in 1625, the deputy lieutenants were reprimanded by the Lord Lieutenant because the King did not believe that they had followed the "printed books" sent to them at the last muster. Some of these manuals were read, however, and elements from them do appear in the few handwritten manuals that still exist (see the appendices in this book).

The handwritten manuals had one big drawback: there were no printed illustrations, and they were one-offs. Any illustrations they did contain were hand drawn and poor quality. It should be noted that not all the printed manuals contained illustrations of the exercises: Edward Cooke's published in 1626 being one example and Markham's, published in 1639, being another.

The advantage of a training manual with pictures as well as text meant that a soldier, in theory, could teach himself how to use his arms. Simply reading how to do it was sometimes not enough, to quote the old saying, "a picture is worth a thousand words".

The downside of a printed manual containing illustrations and written instructions is that it cost more money than most soldiers could afford; handwritten notes were much cheaper and many trained band soldiers could read and write. Would someone who had just bought an expensive book take it to a training day or days, where it could get lost or damaged? A set of cheap, handwritten notes on the other hand were more easily replaced.

Prime y^r Pann

5

Hould y^r touch box betweene y^e thumbe
and forefinger of the right hand
only and ſoe Prime as in y^e figur

1

The Stuart Trained Bands of England and Wales, 1603–1642

The aim of this book is to shed some light on a little-recognised organisation, the early Stuart trained bands, hopefully dispelling some of the myths that exist partly due to the lack of easily accessible information. The intention is to show that by 1642 the trained bands had become a credible force; they possessed the men, arms and armour sufficient for their intended task, they were trained and equipped and a viable, home defence force, although not the "perfect militia" that had been hoped for.

The trained bands were introduced by Elizabeth I in 1572 in an attempt to modernise the country's military strength in the face of threats from Europe, primarily Spain. By 1603, the year of the accession of James I to the English throne, the trained bands were not the force that they had been or were intended to be. Although the external threats were still there, they were not considered to be of current importance, and with a Scottish King on the throne, any threat from Scotland was also removed leaving no direct threats to the country. So, was the state of the trained bands a problem?

In the first half of the seventeenth century with no standing army in this country, its defence would have rested fairly and squarely on the shoulders of the trained bands, as in Elizabethan times. Some men were not convinced that the trained band soldiers could face an experienced Continental army in the field and thought that in the event of an invasion the martial abilities and fervour of the local population would be enough to repel the invaders and that the trained bands were an expensive luxury.[1] The Norfolk deputy lieutenants said as much to the Lord Lieutenant in 1626. Today the style of warfare they advocated might be called guerrilla warfare or more probably, asymmetrical warfare. Those with experience of the fighting on the Continent knew differently. After the accession of James I to the English throne in 1603 the threat of a Scottish invasion, theoretically, disappeared leaving only the threat of a seaborne invasion, probably on the south coast or less possibly

---

1   Walter Rye, *State Papers Relating to Musters, Beacons, Ship-Money, & etc, In Norfolk, from 1626 chiefly to the beginning of the Civil War* (n.p.: Forgotten Books, 2015), pp.18–19.

on the east coast. The Gunpowder Plot in 1605, the ongoing war in the Low Countries, the outbreak of the Thirty Years' War in 1618 and Charles' various ill-advised attempts at military intervention on the Continent showed the military weakness of this country; a military weakness that both James and Charles attempted to rectify during their respective reigns. What followed was the idea of the "Perfect or Exact Militia", the attempt to modernise and discipline the county trained bands. The perception of the trained bands being of little military value comes from a number of sources, the main one seeming to be the *Calendar of State Papers, Domestic*, for the reigns of both James I and Charles I. At the start of Charles' reign it was written in one source that:

> King *Charles,* in the entrance of his Reign, proceeds with Preparations for a War, begun in his Father's time; the Militia of the Kingdom, through the long continued Peace, was much decayed, and the Musters of the trained bands were slighted, and seldom taken, and few of the Commons were expert in the use of Arms; wherefore the Lord Lieutenants were commanded, by Order of the Council, to make a general Muster of the Trained Horse and Foot in the several Counties, and to see to the sufficiency of the Men, Horse, and Arms, and that all be complete according to the best modern form, and be in readiness for all occasions, and especially now the affairs of *Christendom* stand upon such uncertain terms; and more particularly, that the Maritime Towns be well manned, and their Men duly exercised: and the King declared his will and pleasure, that the Lords Lieutenants of the several Shires, should have the nomination of their Deputy Lieutenants.[2]

Charles' intention to create a "Perfect or Exact Militia" should not be doubted and he did have support, at least from the members of his Privy Council. In a letter sent from Edward Conway, Lord Lieutenant of Hampshire to his deputy lieutenants on 24 November 1625, he spoke of Charles' great desire to establish an "Exact Militia".[3] He wanted Hampshire to take the lead in perfecting its trained band, and it should be noted here that the county had one of the largest trained bands and being a coastal county was considered to be at risk of invasion. In his letter Conway emphasised that they would have his full support regarding the trained bands. He would do all that he could to help in their efforts and promised that the King would know of their work. Later in January 1626, Lord Conway wrote to his Deputies again. He informed them that he had passed on their returns to the King and the Privy Council they had been well received.

One of the many problems with the trained bands, and a very important one, was the issue of their legality. Although the trained bands were raised in Elizabeth's reign their legal basis was the legislation introduced in the reign of Philip and Mary which replaced Edward I's Statutes of Winchester dating to 1285. This latter statute stipulated that:

---

2   <https://www.british-history.ac.uk/rushworth-papers/vol1/pp165-219>, accessed 30 November 2019.

3   Hampshire Record Office, 44M69/G5/37/1/1.

It is likewise commanded that every man have in his house arms for keeping the peace in accordance with the ancient assize; namely that every man between fifteen years and sixty be assessed and sworn to arms according to the amount of his lands and, of his chattels; that is to say:

For fifteen pounds of land, and, forty marks worth of chattels, a hauberk, a helmet of iron, a sword, a knife and a horse.

For ten pounds worth of land and, twenty marks worth of chattels, a haubergeon, a helmet, a sword and a knife; for a hundred shillings worth of land, a doublet, a helmet of iron, a sword and a knife.

For forty shillings worth of land and over, up to a hundred shillings worth, a sword, a bow, arrows and a knife.

He who has less than forty shillings worth of land shall be sworn to have scythes. gisarrnes, knives and other small weapons.

He who has less than twenty marks in chattels, swords, knives and other small weapons.

And all others who can do so shall have bows and arrows outside the forests and within them bows and bolts.

And that the view of arms was to be made twice a year. And in each hundred and liberty let two constables be chosen to make the view of arms and the aforesaid constables shall, when the justices assigned to this come to the district, present before them the defaults they have found in arms, in watch-keeping and in highways.

As already noted, this statute was repealed by Philip and Mary in 1558 and replaced by a new one. This introduced a rating system based on a man's wealth, in land or goods, and this determined what arms and armour he was charged with. Tables 1 and 2 (end of chapter) show the rating systems used.

The statute of Philip and Mary was itself repealed by James I in 1604 but was not replaced with new legislation, thus the Statutes of Winchester were considered by some to have come back into force. However, this was not accepted by everyone and caused the legal basis of the trained bands to be questioned on a number of occasions.

Another major problem was the payment of the county muster master. Under Elizabeth this post had been financed by central government, and when this burden was passed on to the counties there was dissension. The counties had not been consulted on the matter and most either did not pay or paid reluctantly and usually in arrears. Some of the men who filled these posts were well-qualified and experienced soldiers, others however were servants of the lord lieutenant. Some lord lieutenants were accused of using the county to pay for their own servants, an accusation that could not be simply ignored and in some cases was quite possibly true.

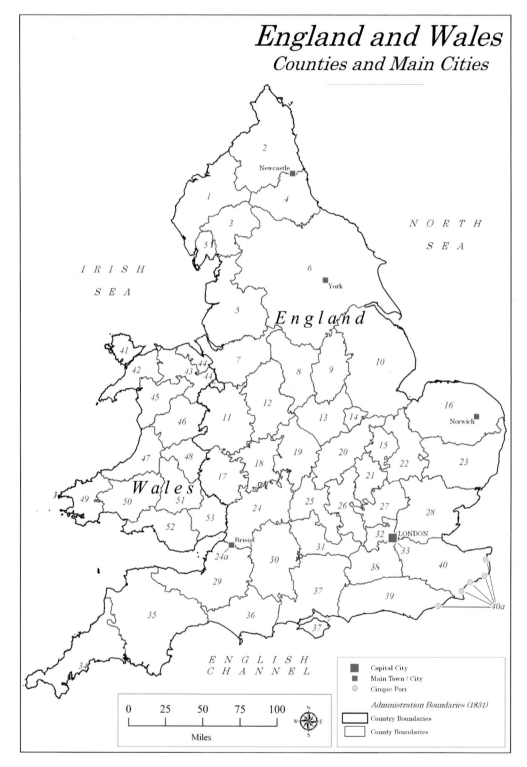

Map 1. County map of England and Wales showing the counties as they were in the seventeenth century, see Table 3, p.16. (Mapping software kindly provided by the Cambridge Group, the ESRC, the Leverhulme Trust and the British Academy and produced by Derek Tate)

Despite all the issues concerning the trained bands there is one highly relevant point: that is, the actual numbers of men enrolled in the trained bands. In one of the Essex Lieutenancy books is a table giving the numbers of each county's trained band.[4] The county totals are dated between 1615 and 1625. These figures are of interest when looked at with the data given for the trained bands prior to the 1st Bishops' War, 1639; both sets of figures are shown below. The first point to make is that the figures from Essex for each county are dated somewhere between 1615 and 1625 for each county, the year is included. The second point is that the overall totals for the two sets of figures are comparable although three of the counties did not have any figures shown against them for either source. These were Cumberland, Northumberland and Westmorland, the Middle Shires. Some of the counties in the first set appear to include the trained and untrained soldiers; this is definitely the case for Rutland. While Leicestershire, which had combined its common and private soldiers into a single regiment in 1588, has a note in both tables saying that they had 500 trained soldiers and another 500 private soldiers available. Finally, in the first set the soldiers from the Cinque Ports, the Isle of Wight and the Stannaries are not included; in the second list those from the Cinque Ports are included but not the other two. The Isle of Wight has approximately 2,000 men available. Both sets of data are shown in Table 3 (end of chapter). A map has been included (facing page) as some of these counties no longer exist in the same form today as they did in the seventeenth century.

By the start of the Bishops' Wars the trained bands, horse and foot, in England and Wales numbered approximately 100,000 men, armed, equipped, organised and trained. Admittedly their level of training was variable, but trained they were and they were definitely armed and equipped, or at least the foot were. The horse were a different matter, as will be seen. Looking at the numbers it becomes obvious why control of the trained bands was one of the major issues between the Parliament and the King prior to the Civil War. Table 3 and Map 1 show how unevenly the trained band soldiers were distributed around the country. This was something that was unavoidable. By 1638 the actual reported numbers per county were as shown in Table 4 (end of chapter).[5]

Three counties did not provide numbers for their trained bands: these were Cumberland, Northumberland and Westmorland. These had previously been ordered to raise and train 500 foot and 100 horse within the county of Northumberland and a further 500 foot from the town of Newcastle, the counties of Cumberland and Westmorland were to jointly raise 500 foot and 100 horse. Some of these troops were raised, but which and how many remains open to discussion.

It should be mentioned that the trained bands were backed up by the untrained bands in many counties and the freeholder bands in some towns. Partly and usually poorly armed and equipped and sometimes partly trained

4   Bodleian Library MS Firth, c4.
5   The National Archives, SP16/381

but often organised, they were another resource that was intended to be used in a crisis.

Were the trained bands ever put to the test in combat? Prior to the Civil War they did not fight. They were called upon in the 1st Bishops' War but no fighting took place. After the disaster at Newburn, Charles wanted the trained bands brought into the field but would they have fought? This is a matter of conjecture; the present author believes that given the motivation they would have fought and fought well. The question is, what would have motivated them?

Table 1. Rating system for contributions to maintain trained band soldiers – lands

Every person temporal shall keep that which hath estate of inheritance on freehold in lands etc.											
Estate	Horses or geldings, demi-lances with armour for them, whereof the one half shall be horses, at the least with furniture	Light horses with their furniture of harness & weapon	Corslets furnished	Almain rivets, plate coats, brigandines or corslets furnished	Pikes	Longbows	Sheaves of arrows	Steel caps of sculls	Black bills or halberds	Harquebuts	Morions or sallets
£1,000	6	10	40	40	40	30	30	30	20	20	20
1,000 marks	4	6	30	30	30	20	20	20	10	10	10
£400	2	4	20	20	20	15	15	15		6	6
£200	1	2	10	10	10	8	8	8		3	3
£100		2	3	3	3	3	3	3		2	2
100 marks		1	2	2	2	2	2	2		1	1
£40			2	2	2	1	1	1		1	1
£20			1		1	1	1	1		1	1
£10				1		1	1	1		1	1
£5				1		1	1	1	1		

Table 2. Rating system for contributions to maintain trained band soldiers – goods

Every person temporal shall keep that which hath estate of inheritance in goods											
Estate	Horses or geldings, demi-lances with armour for them, whereof the one half shall be horses, at the least with furniture	Light horses with their furniture of harness & weapon	Corslets furnished	Almain rivets, plate coats, brigandines or corslets furnished	Pikes	Longbows	Sheaves of arrows	Steel caps of sculls	Black bills or halberds	Harquebuts	Morions or sallets
1,000 marks	*1	1	2	2	2	4	4	4		3	3
£400		*2	1	2	1	2	2	2		1	
£200			1	2	1	2	2	2		1	
£100			1	1	1	2	2	2		1	1
£40				2		1	1	1	1		
£20				1		2	2	2	1		
£10						1	1	1	1		

*1: In the place of horsemen those with estates valued in goods were to provide 18 corslets, furnished
*2: In the place of light horsemen those with estates valued in goods were to provide 9 corslets, furnished

Table 3. Trained band numbers by county, 1615–1625 (see Map 1, p.12)

Key	County	Country	Year	Foot	Horse
1	Cumberland	England			
2	Northumberland	England			
3	Westmorland	England			
4	Durham	England	1620	1,000	100
5	Lancashire	England	1625	7,193*	109
6	Yorkshire	England	1615	12,000	0
7	Cheshire	England	1625	1,100	66
8	Derbyshire	England	1625	848	74
9	Nottinghamshire	England	1625	1,025	60
10	Lincolnshire	England	1622	2,280	269
11	Shropshire	England	1625	600	100
12	Staffordshire	England	1619	400	100
13	Leicestershire	England	1625	500*	80
14	Rutland	England	1625	173*	27
15	Huntingdonshire	England	1620	400	50
16	Norfolk	England	1619	4,184	320
17	Herefordshire	England	1625	480	81
18	Worcestershire	England	1624	650	70
19	Warwickshire	England	1625	600	100
20	Northamptonshire	England	1625	1,286	221
21	Bedfordshire	England	1623	620	70
22	Cambridgeshire	England	1619	300	107
23	Suffolk	England	1615	3,782	145
24	Gloucestershire	England	1625	325*	220
24a	Bristol	England			
25	Oxfordshire	England	1619	950	80
26	Buckinghamshire	England	1619	800	102
27	Hertfordshire	England	1623	1,650	80
28	Essex	England	1620	3,820	172
29	Somerset	England	1624	5,000	300
30	Wiltshire	England	1624	2,455	137
31	Berkshire	England	1619	1,000	80
32	Middlesex	England	1615	1,523	60
33	London	England			
34	Cornwall	England	1624	3,840	0
35	Devonshire	England	1624	5,819	150

Key	County	Country	Year	Foot	Horse
36	Dorsetshire	England	1619	3,429	100
37	Hampshire	England	1622	5329	158
38	Surrey	England	1621	1500	145
39	Sussex	England	1621	4437	36
40	Kent	England	1621	4259	232
40a	Cinque Ports	England			
41	Anglesey	Wales	1625	400	0
42	Caernarvon	Wales	1625	200	16
43	Denbigh	Wales	1625	200	30
44	Flint	Wales	1625	200	30
45	Merioneth	Wales	1625	200	0
46	Montgomery	Wales	1625	200	30
47	Cardigan	Wales	1625	300	0
48	Radnor	Wales	1625	200	35
49	Pembroke	Wales	1625	600	200
50	Carmarthen	Wales	1625	450	0
51	Brecknock	Wales	1625	300	50
52	Glamorgan	Wales	1620	400	35
53	Monmouth	Wales	1620	600	47

* = Figures do include the untrained men. The asterisk against Gloucestershire shows an error in the original document which has not been corrected, as the correction would have to be an informed guess.

Table 4. Trained band numbers by county, 1638

Counties	Foot			Horse					
	M	C*	Total	La	Cu	LH	Ha	Dr	Total
Anglesey	259	141	400						25
Bedfordshire	296	204	500	40		30			70
Berkshire	680	420	1,100		59		31		90
Breconshire	180	120	300						30
Bristol	210	90	300						0
Buckinghamshire	400	200	600	47	55				102
Cambridgeshire	540	460	1,000		30			50	80
Cardigan	150	150	300						35
Carmarthen	220	330*	550						35

Counties	Foot			Horse					
	M	C*	Total	La	Cu	LH	Ha	Dr	Total
Carnarvon	100	100	200						25
Cheshire	360	240	600						
Cinque Ports	1,649	326	1,975						14
Cornwall	3,850	2,310	6,160						0
Cumberland									
Derbyshire	239	161	400		33			41	74
Denbigh	300	200	500						50
Devonshire	4,253	2,509	6,702						126
Dorset	1,444	696	2,140						100
Durham	532	500	1,032						60
Essex	2,152	1,878	4,030	50		200			250
Flintshire	140	60	200						30
Glamorgan	200	200	400						36
Gloucestershire	1,826	1,294	3,120						200
Hampshire	2,854	1,945	4,799						170
Hertfordshire	750	750	1,500	27		53			80
Herefordshire	280	200	480						90
Huntingdonshire	240	160	400	20		30			50
Kent	2,910	1,757	4,667						293
Lancashire	420	180	600	25		81			106
Leicestershire	290	210	500	38		62			100
Lincolnshire	1,080	720	1,800						230
London	3,000	3,000	6,000						0
Merioneth	100	100	200						15
Middlesex	928	653	1,581						80
Monmouthshire	200	200	400						47
Montgomery	150	150	300						50
Norfolk	2,910	2,407	5,317		80		320		400
Northamptonshire	284	295	579	58		50			108
Northumberland									
Nottinghamshire	282	125	407		50			10	60
Oxfordshire	500	350	850	40		40			80
Pembrokeshire	276	281	557						57
Radnor	112	88	200						25
Rutland	60	40	100			30			30
Shropshire	341	259	600						100
Somerset	2,403	1,597	4,000		82		218		300

Counties	Foot			Horse						
	M	C*	Total	La	Cu	LH	Ha	Dr	Total	
Staffordshire	248	152	400		73	30			103	
Suffolk	2,359	1,789	4,148		300				300	
Surrey	604	896	1,500		63		66		129	
Sussex	1,804	1,000	2,804						160	
Warwickshire	357	243	600		88				88	
Westmorland										
Worcestershire	491	309	800						70	
Wiltshire	1,285	1,115	2,400	30		126			156	
Yorkshire	6,720	5,521	12,241		365			35	400	
Written Totals	54,517	39,081*	93,718						5,239	
Actual Totals			93,239						5,309	

*This includes armoured and unarmoured pikemen

The troop types are M=musketeer, C=corslet, La=lancer, Cu=cuirassier, LH=light horse, Ha=harquebusier, Dr=dragoon

Shut y^r Pann

6

Lay y^r thumbe over the barrell neare the Pann, and with your two formost fingers, shut the Pann

2

The Regimental and Company Organisations for the Trained Bands, Foot and Horse

There were no national Tables of Organisation and Equipment (TO&E) for the trained bands, foot or horse, during the reigns of either James or Charles. The nearest that the trained bands came to a national organisation was the use of foot companies and horse troops as the basic units in the trained bands of each county. Each county had its own TO&E for the foot companies and the horse troops, sometimes there was standardisation between the companies and the regiments, where there were regiments, within a county and sometimes there was not. Two contrasting examples here are the county of Hampshire and the City of London. In Hampshire, at the start of James' reign, there were seven foot divisions and four companies raised by the towns of Southampton and Winchester. By late 1625 or early 1626 the divisions had become regiments, these and the four companies raised by the towns of Southampton and Winchester meant that there was a total of 45 foot companies in the county. The organisation of the seven divisions/regiments changed between the years 1619 and 1627, despite using the same geographical names. The number of foot companies the divisions/regiments had in 1619 and 1627 gives a good idea of some of the changes, see Table 5. The divisions had colonels in charge but there does not seem to have been a lieutenant colonel or sergeant-major in them as there were later on with the regiments.[1]

Each of the Hampshire foot companies was of an irregular size and composition. There was no laid down TO&E for these companies.

In London there were four foot regiments, each with 1,500 men, and each regiment was ordered to have five companies. By 1638 these were equally divided between musketeers and pikemen. This uniform organisation was used from at least 1608 until the outbreak of the Civil War. The only changes noted were the recruiting areas for the various companies, a complete contrast to Hampshire.

---

1 British Library Add MS 21922.

Table 5. Number of foot companies in the Hampshire divisions/regiments in 1619 and 1627

	Division (1619)	Regiment (1627)
Alton	6	6
Andover	9	7
Basingstoke	8	7
Fawley	3	3
Kingsclere	3	6
New Forest	7	7
Portsdown	5	5

The horse in the counties were organised into individual troops although there is some evidence for the existence of a small regiment being formed in Somerset. These county organisations did not change very much if at all, over this period, the numbers did vary but usually by not by very much. The type of horseman fielded by the counties did change though, as will be discussed later.

Despite manuals being issued which called for companies of 100 men and regiments of 1,000 men, none of the counties actually followed this organisation.[2] Some counties did have companies that were 100 men strong but did not have regiments of 1,000 men. Even counties with the same lord lieutenant did not have the same regimental organisation. Edward Seymour, 1st Earl of Hertford was the lord lieutenant of Somerset, Wiltshire and the city of Bristol from 1601 until his death in 1621. Somerset had four foot regiments, each of 800 men organised into six captain's companies of 100 men and the colonel's company of 200 men. Wiltshire also had four foot regiments but these numbered 600 men each, comprising four captain's companies of 100 men and the colonel's company of 200 men, and Bristol had three companies of 100 men each.

The ratios of pike to shot also varied in the training manuals that were used. *The Military Garden* by James Achesone, printed in 1629, called for companies of 200 men with equal number of pikemen and musketeers as did an undated manual from Derbyshire.[3] Not surprisingly the ratios of shot to pike varied between the counties and the companies within regiments within the same county. In Hampshire the ratio of pike versus shot for the county in 1626 was 42 percent to 58 percent, the next year this was 41 percent to 59 percent, however, the ratios between companies varied greatly, Sir John Compton's company in the Alton Regiment had a ratio of 36 percent pike to 64 percent shot while Sir White Beconsawe's company in the New Forest Regiment had a ratio of 57 percent pike to 43 percent shot.[4] One company in the Portsdown Regiment in Hampshire was entirely armed with muskets

---

2 The 1623 manual authorised by the Privy Council actually called for companies of 100 men without specifying the number of pikemen or musketeers or mentioning regiments.
3 Derbyshire Record Office, D2375-m-36-17.
4 British Library Add MS 21922, folio 5.

but this was earmarked to reinforce the garrison at Hurst Castle where pikes would have been something of a liability.

Attempts to achieve some sort of standardisation were made. On 23 June 1617 Lord Gerard, Lord Lieutenant of Shropshire, wrote to Sir Robert Needham and Sir Robert Vernon, two of his deputies.[5] He wrote that he wanted the soldiers in the trained band to be equipped and organised as he had previously ordered and for this to be done by 1 October. Specifically, he wanted every 100 men to be armed in the following ratio: 40 men with corslets and pikes, 28 musketeers complete with wooden bandoleers, 28 bastard musketeers with wooden bandoleers, and four men with swords and targets. In 1625 the foot in the Shropshire Trained Band numbered 600 men, organised into four companies of 150 men each.[6] These men were reported to be organised in four companies in 1635 by the muster master, Edward Burton, with the number of musketeers being about 320 which would mean approximately 280 pikemen.[7] These numbers remained the same until at least February 1638, when they were again reported as 600 foot made up of 341 musketeers and 259 pikemen.[8] Converting the numbers from 1617 would give totals of 240 pikemen and 336 musketeers with 24 other men, formerly armed with swords and targets, later converted to either pike or shot. A comparison of these two sets of figures gives us percentages of 40 percent pike, 56 percent shot and four percent other in 1617, and 43 percent pike and 57 percent shot in 1638. These two sets of figures are definitely comparable to each other.

The issue of standardisation was appreciated at all levels. In 1635 the Council of War issued a set of instructions which included how it thought a company of horse should be organised.[9] A company should number 100 men; this would include the captain, lieutenant, cornet, quartermaster, three corporals, two trumpeters, clerk, saddler, surgeon, farrier and 90 troopers. The company should be divided into three equally sized squadrons of 30 troopers, the first led by the captain, the second by the cornet and the third by the senior corporal. When the company formed up the squadrons should be in files five deep which would give a frontage of six men per squadron and 18 for the company. The lieutenant and quartermaster were placed at the rear of the squadron.

So what actual organisation did exist within each county?

The Foot Companies

We know from documentary evidence that the men were organised into companies for the foot, each company having a geographical recruiting area, the company was the basic tactical and administrative unit for the foot. Each foot company contained a number of officers; these were the captain,

5   Historical Manuscripts Commission, *Tenth report of the Royal Commission on Historical Manuscripts* (London: Eyre & Spottiswoode, 1885), p.365.
6   Bodleian Library MS Firth c4.
7   Huntington Library, California University, Bridgwater Collection EL 7673.
8   Calendar of State Papers, Domestic Series, SP 16/381 dated 9th February 1638.
9   Rye, *State Papers Relating to Musters*, pp.201–2.

lieutenant and ensign or ancient. Every foot company, in every county, had these three men, or were supposed to have them. In addition to these three officers there were a number of sergeants, who were classed as officers, there were also corporals and musicians, these being drummers and sometimes, fifers. One other rank existed and this was the lansprisado, often noted as a pikeman, but not always, while the corporal was usually with the musketeers. The rank of lansprisado was not used by all the counties and does not seem to have been in continuous use. Some companies also had clerks, armourers and some even had their own surgeon. The numbers of sergeants and corporals varied and it would seem to have been the captain's decision on how many he had in his company despite various manuals stating the number that there should be. The rank and file of the company was divided into pike and shot; having said that, some companies also possessed small numbers of halberdiers although their role varied and in James' time, some also had a few men armed with sword and shield or target. Each foot company was then, according to the manuals, sub-divided into three squadrons; these are referred to in some documents as "corporalships".[10] Despite what the manuals said, this company level organisation was not always followed.

We have a number of examples of the actual organisation of some foot companies; these have come from the surviving muster rolls for those companies. The information for them is as follows.

The first muster roll comes from Anglesey, dated 25 September 1616, and was for a muster of the trained band of the Talybolion Commote in Anglesey,[11] one of six foot companies on the island, and it gives the company's organisation. Before 1619, the shot within the company would have been comprised of men armed with calivers or muskets. This is the only document the present author has found that shows the integration of both types of these firearms within a company, a company with a very irregular organisation.

The names of all the company members with their allotted weapons and roles were included in the muster roll. The three officers were Captain Hugh Owen, Lieutenant Hugh Bulkeley and Ensign John Griffith. Also in this company were three sergeants, Richard Griffith, Rowland Owen and John ap Hugh, a drummer, Robert Jones and Richard Bulkeley, the company's clerk. For the muster the company was listed in the muster roll by squadrons of which there were 12. One squadron was comprised of a number of gentlemen, while each of the other 11 squadrons was armed with a particular weapon type, shot or polearm, and numbered up to 22 men each. The squadron composed of gentlemen numbered 12 men who were supposed to carry swords and targets but any other weapons would seem to have sufficed, and they were to guard the company colour and the captain and to lead files and soldiers as required. Another four gentlemen, not seemingly part of the company, were supposed to wear their own armour and trail pikes, "as they wished"; although oddly one of these gentlemen was noted as being armed with a musket and another with a caliver. Four of the squadrons were

10 Derbyshire Record Office, D2375-m-36-17.
11 National Library of Wales, Carreglwyd Estate Records, Talybolion Hundred, 25th September 1616.

predominantly pike armed and seven were shot, each of the companies had a corporal and a lansprisado and 17–20 men. There were variations in the actual armour that the men in each of the squadrons wore and the arms they carried, including the corporals and lansprisados, these were as follows:

1st (Pike) Squadron, 7 men with pike and corslet, 10 men with pike, burgonet and sword, 2 men with pike and sword, 2 men with pikes and 1 man with a bill.

2nd (Pike) Squadron, 6 men with pike and corslet, 14 men with pike, burgonet and sword, 1 man with a pike and burgonet and 1 man with a bill and sword.

3rd (Pike) Squadron, 5 men with pike and corslet, 6 men with pike, burgonet and sword, 1 man with pike and sword, 6 men with pikes and 1 man with a bill.

4th (Pike) Squadron, 4 men with pike and corslet, 11 men with pike, burgonet and sword, 2 men with pike and burgonet, 1 man with a pike and sword, 1 man with a bill and sword and 1 man with a bill.

1st (Shot) Squadron, 7 men with muskets, 6 men with calivers and targets, 4 men with calivers and another item and 3 men with calivers.

2nd (Shot) Squadron, 8 men with muskets, 5 men with calivers and targets, 1 man with a caliver and another item and 6 men with calivers.

3rd (Shot) Squadron, 7 men with muskets, 7 men with calivers and targets and 6 men with calivers.

4th (Shot) Squadron, 12 men with muskets, 2 men with calivers and targets, 1 man with a caliver and another item and 5 men with calivers.

5th (Shot) Squadron, 8 men with muskets, 7 men with calivers and targets and 3 men with calivers. The equipment of the corporal and lansprisado is not known for this squadron.

6th (Shot) Squadron, 8 men with muskets, 5 men with calivers and targets and 7 men with calivers.

7th (Shot) Squadron, 8 men with muskets, 4 men with calivers and targets, 2 men with calivers and another item and 6 men with calivers.

There are a number of points to note with this company's organisation. The first is that this organisation, although this is not stated, includes both the trained and untrained men. There were 83 pike and billmen, 225 shot and the 16 gentlemen. This company mustered 21 pikemen and 56 musketeers, trained soldiers, in the late 1630s. The second is that each of the squadrons equates to a "corporalship" of approximately 20 men, including the corporal and the lansprisado. The corporal and lansprisado were not always the best-equipped men within their squadrons. Also, the role of the gentlemen should not be forgotten. When they were not protecting the captain or the colours, it may be that they were intended to act as "stiffeners" to the soldiers or replacements for the corporals and lansprisados if they became casualties.

The requirements of Lord Gerard, Lord Lieutenant of Shropshire, regarding the equipping and organising of the county's trained band, have already been noted. Shrewsbury's Trained Band included two men armed with targets until at least 1622, by 1626 they were no longer listed.[12] This the county had achieved by 1638 if not sooner although the sword- and target-armed men had been converted to muskets by then.

The Sussex musters of 1618 contain information on the required organisation of the foot companies.[13] The muster master issued a set of rules for the selected bands, however there is no evidence that these requirements were met. The first rule was that each company should be made even in number. This probably meant that each company should contain the same number of men; the figure given was 168 men except for the Chichester Company which numbered 150. The second rule was that every company was to be organised into squadrons and files. Every 40 men were to be under the command of a corporal, he was to have three file leaders under him and they were each to lead a file consisting of themselves and nine men.

In 1619 the town and port of Hythe, one of the Cinque Ports, fielded a trained band company of 96 soldiers comprised of 32 pikemen and 64 musketeers.[14] The company officers at this time were Captain John Hales, Gentleman Lieutenant Thomas Browning, Ensign James Fordred, Sergeant Reignold and Drummer Thomas Lynett. The 96 soldiers appear to have been organised into six units, each of 16 men and each under the command of a corporal. Each of these units was armed with either a pike or a musket. The four corporals in charge of the musketeers were John Browning, Richard Evering, Richard Lyndson and Thomas Sydney; the two corporals in charge of the pikes were Thomas Culling and Michael Prowde.

The next example of a company organisation also dates to 1619. The foot company was that of Sandwich, Kent, one of the Cinque Ports, the three officers were Captain Joshua Pordage,[15] Lieutenant George Wood and Richard Luck, the ensign. There were also two sergeants, Josias Ent and John Gason, and three musicians, John Burton, the drummer, and two fifers, Henry Parker and Nicholas Hayward. In 1619 the company also had Raphe Sumner as its clerk and Charles Annet as its surgeon. There were also eight corporals, Thomas Greensted, William Richardson, John Peak and Thomas Henaken with the pikes and John Halsnod, William Elwood, William Ladd and John Solmar with the muskets. The company included 63 pikemen

---

12   Shropshire Record Office, 3365/2563/1-4.
13   Sussex Record Office, Sussex Archaeological Collections, Vol. XL, p.119.
14   The National Archives, SP 14/108, f.13.
15   British Library Add MS 33511, folio 208, and The National Archives, SP 14/108, f. 25a.

and 84 musketeers, this works out at one corporal for every 16 pikemen and one for every 21 musketeers, including the corporals. These figures are comparable to those for Anglesey even if the organisation is not.

In the same year, 1619, the muster for Dover's Selected Band or Company, again one of the Cinque Ports, gives a breakdown of its organisation.[16] The three officers were Captain Francis Wilsford, Esq., Lieutenant James Hughessen, and Ensign John Bing. In addition there were three sergeants Edward Grant, William Waad and John Jenkins, Drummer Henry Barnes, Fifer Henry Wyldes and Surgeon Thomas Day. There were also four corporals and four lansprisados, two of each for the shot and the pikemen. For the shot were Corporals Thomas Sweeting and John Smyth, and Lansprisados John Badgent and Roger Smyth, and for the pikemen there were Corporals Robert Kennett and Richard Golder and Lansprisados John Pett and John Eger. In the company were 80 armoured pikemen (corslets) and 80 musketeers, also contained within their ranks were a number of men entitled "Gentlemen of the Company", eight with the musketeers and four with the pikemen. The division of the soldiers within this company is open to conjecture. Two corporals and two lansprisados for 80 soldiers could mean two "corporalships" or four "corporalships" if the lansprisados are used. Also, the role of the "Gentlemen of the Company" is not clear at all.

The muster roll for the select band of Winchelsea, another town of the Cinque Ports, dated 25 March 1619, gives a total of 12 pikemen and 31 musketeers listed on the muster roll as well as the officers.[17] Some of the musketeers were noted as carrying snaphances instead of muskets at this muster. All those with firearms were issued with a full proportion of powder and bullets and for those with muskets, a length of match as well. The three officers were Captain William Wymonde, formerly the Lieutenant, Lieutenant Paul Wymonde and Ensign John Collins; there was also a musician, Drummer Bartholomew John Cocke. There were also three corporals, one for the pikemen and two for the musketeers. The musketeers were listed in two blocks with one corporal and 14 men in one block and a corporal and 15 men in the other block.

In Hampshire in 1626, the Crondall and Bentley Company of the Basingstoke Regiment held a muster.[18] The company was commanded by Sir Walter Tichborne of Aldershot, MP, who was also the regiment's lieutenant colonel. In 1626 the company's muster roll listed the officers and included a breakdown of the roles the soldiers were allocated in the field. These roles were file leaders, middlemen and bringer-ups, the files numbered between nine and 11 men each. The company included 37 pikemen and 41 musketeers from a number of locations. The pikemen were organised into one file of 10 men, a file leader, eight other men including middlemen and a bringer-up, and three files of nine men, one of these had a file leader and eight other men including middlemen while the other two had a file leader, seven other men including middlemen and a bringer-up. The size

16   The National Archives, SP 14/108, f.4.
17   The National Archives, SP 14/107, f.81.
18   Hampshire Militia Muster Rolls, number 13, transcribed and published by Mike Barnes, 2008.

of the files indicates that a training manual was probably being followed. There is no mention of corporals or lansprisados being part of the company although this does not mean that they were not there, possibly they were simply not identified.

Also in 1626 and again in Hampshire the Twyford Company of the Fawley Regiment held a muster.[19] The company at this time was commanded by Captain Edward Seymour,[20] and the muster roll for the company was submitted by Seymour on 10 August 1626 as part of the regimental muster. Besides the usual information on the soldiers, the roll also details which of the men are designated as file leaders, middlemen and bringers-up, both for the musketeers and the pikemen. Of the 71 musketeers six were file leaders, 10 were middlemen and six were bringers-up. Theoretically this could indicate six files of at least 11–12 men in each. Of the 47 pikemen four were file leaders, eight were middlemen and four were bringers-up. Again, theoretically this indicates four files of at least 11–12 men in each. Having said that, we have to allow for absent soldiers and there were eight pikemen and 12 musketeers noted as being defective or absent, this would give 10 files of 10 men including the file leaders, the bringers-up and the middlemen. The four files of pikemen would have had two middlemen while the six files of musketeers would have been short of two middlemen.

The Suffolk muster returns for 1631 give the strengths of two of the foot companies, one of 200 men and the other, Captain Roger North's Company, of 239 men. North's company in 1631 comprised three officers, North himself, Lieutenant John Soame, gent and Ensign Thomas Potter, gent.; there were four sergeants, Thomas Crispe, Thomas Childerston, John Collison and William Cowell and four corporals William Potter, John Gillye, Henry Keene and John Nelson. The company also had two drummers John Coppen and Rowland Bull. The company was comprised of 112 pikemen and 127 musketeers.[21] The large number of men and the small number of corporals is surprising, approximately 60 men per corporal. This would seem to indicate a difference in their role. This may have been something unique to Suffolk or a change which affected the whole system.

Two documents from Yorkshire dated to 1633 give some information on the hierarchical structure for the foot companies in at least the West Riding. Each of the companies was to have a captain, a lieutenant, two sergeants, three corporals and two drummers.[22] One of the documents goes on to state that the soldiers were to be organised into files of 10 men each.

A comparison between the numbers of men provided by the same county is worthwhile; the Yorkshire wapentakes were fairly consistent over a number of years. Morley Wapentake, West Riding, provided 183 pikemen, 90 musketeers and 134 calivermen, (a total of 224 shot), in 1602, all common soldiers. In 1625 they provided 188 pikemen and 213 musketeers, all common soldiers. It should be pointed out that a further 415 private soldiers

---

19   Hampshire Militia Muster Rolls, Number 19 transcribed and published by Mike Barnes, 2009.
20   Sir Henry Withed's Letter Book, Volume 1, 1601–14, Hampshire Record Office, 1976, pp.27–28.
21   The National Archives, SP 16/201, f.70
22   West Yorkshire Archives Service, 32D86/38, folio 41, and the British Library, Add Ch 39546.

were also provided. The men provided in 1625 and 1638 by the combined Wapentakes of Strafforth & Tickhill, West Riding, were also comparable, 45 pikemen in 1625 and 47 in 1638, and 74 musketeers in 1625 and 76 in 1638.

The Troop Bands or Untrained Men

The troop bands were untrained, ill-equipped but with some organisation. They were called different names in different counties. The men were selected from the county-wide musters of all able-bodied men aged between 16 and 60 years of age.

By 1615 Lancashire had organised its untrained men into regiments based on the county's hundreds.[23] These were regiments in name only but did have the men under captains with their own companies. Both the regiments and their subordinate companies were of an irregular size. The Lancashire return for the untrained men in 1628 is shown in Table 6:

Included in the muster instructions for Devon in 1620 was an item concerning the organisation of the county's untrained men.[24] The colonels of every regiment were to appoint captains and other officers for the untrained bands, allotting to each captain 200 men who were as speedily as possible to see the soldiers sufficiently armed and a roll made. This presumably meant that the regiments in Devon were to have one or more companies of untrained men included in them.

In 1628 the Dorset deputies reported the current state of the county's forces to the Lord Lieutenant.[25] They reported that they had included the troop bands with the trained bands. The troop bands were only mustered twice a year and the arms and armour were mostly obsolete, including calivers and curats provided by men of lesser means, usually grouped three or four together to pay for a musket or a corslet or equivalent. These men had been formed into seven companies of 100 men each. These men probably comprised the county's untrained men.

The Foot Regiments

As has been noted, some counties had sufficient trained men to form regiments within their county; London, Yorkshire, Hampshire, Somerset and Devon, certainly formed regiments. Looking at the county organisations one thing soon becomes apparent: only one county had a regiment with 1,000 men, and that was Leicestershire. However, that regiment had five companies of about 200 men each and not the 100-strong companies advocated. It can be assumed that the county organisations were for peacetime and that should they have been required for war then there would have been a reorganisation for deployment into the field. How this would have been done remains unknown.

23   Lancashire Record Office, DX/2044/11.
24   Devon Heritage Centre, 3799M-3/O/2/41.
25   The National Archives, SP 16/120, f.8.

Table 6. The Lancashire return for the untrained men in 1628

Hundreds	Colonels & Captains	Men	Muskets	Corslets	Bills	Pioneers
Derby	Sir Richard Molyneux, colonel, Sir Charles Gerrard, Thomas Ashlow & Edward Barber, captains	1,922	340	128	130	1,328
Salford	Sir Cecil Trafford, kt, Edward Holland, John Greenhaugh & Leonard Ashawe, captains	1,147	235	106	31	734
Leyland	Sir Gilbert Hoghton, colonel & Thomas Standish, captain	670	96	42	31	496
Blackburn	Sir Raph Asheton, colonel, Rad Asher & John Braddill, captains	1,224	124	64	62	967
Amoundernes	Sir Richard Hoghton, colonel, Tho Hoghton, captain	1,208	168	57	60	903
Lonsdale	Alexander Rigby colonel, Thomas Covelay, captain	1,067	135	55	51	827
		7,238	1,098	452	365	5,255

Regiments for Continental and Home Service

Although the trained bands were intended for home defence, a study of the organisation of the regiments of pressed soldiers sent abroad and the temporary trained band regiments formed in a crisis may be of use.

Despite the many manuals stating regiments of 1,000 men when regiments of levied men were raised and sent abroad many of these were not organised in this required manner either. There are some clues as to how the trained band foot regiments might have been organised when taking to the field. The regiments sent to the Continent were organised before their departure. Their TO&E varied with each expedition, but whether this was intentional, required or just a case of doing the best with what you have, is not known.

In 1621 James I wanted to send an army to the Palatinate to support his brother-in-law, but this project never happened. The planned preparations were documented at a Privy Council Meeting held on 21 January 1621.[26] The TO&E for the foot regiments was 13 companies, the colonel's company being 200 strong, including four gentlemen and four corporals and 12 foot companies of 150 men each, including three gentlemen and three corporals, a total of 2,000 men per regiment. The officers for each regiment included the colonel, a lieutenant colonel, a sergeant major, a quartermaster, a provost, a carriage-master, a preacher and a surgeon. The officers at company level included a captain, a lieutenant, an ensign, two sergeants (three in the colonel's company), two drummers (three in the colonel's company) and a surgeon. The TO&E for the horse was also documented, there were

---

26 D.E. Evans, *Equipping a C17th Army: an estimate of the English forces required for the war in the Palatinate* (Powys: March Publications, 1985).

no regimental organisations, only those for the individual troops. Each troop was to number 100 men plus a captain, a lieutenant, a cornet, three corporals, a quartermaster, a surgeon and two trumpeters. This was a similar organisation proposed by the Council of War in their instruction dated 1635.

Three years later, in 1624, a number of regiments were raised for service on the Continent under Count Mansfeld. These regiments had a standard organisation of 10 companies, a colonel's company, a lieutenant colonel's company and a sergeant major's company, all three comprised of 250 men, and seven other companies of 200 men each making a total of 2,150 men for the regiment.[27]

In 1625 there was a perceived threat of invasion from the Continent. To prevent this, the Privy Council ordered the lord lieutenants of the maritime counties on the south and east coasts and also the counties of Somerset and Pembroke, to ready their trained bands. The Privy Council gave instructions that the soldiers were to be organised into regiments.[28]

In January 1626, 10 more regiments were ordered to be raised. The organisation for these regiments was again different. Each consisted of 10 companies, the colonel's company was to be 200 strong, the lieutenant colonel's company 150 strong, the sergeant major's company 130 strong, and the other seven companies 100 men strong,[29] a total of 1,180 men in each regiment.

The remnants of the 10 regiments raised in 1626 were reorganised in March 1627 into five regiments. Each of these was to be made up of 10 companies with each company having 80 men. This meant the colonel's, lieutenant colonel's and the sergeant major's companies having the same number of men as the seven captain's companies.[30] This new organisation gave each regiment a strength of 800 men each.

There were two additional regiments raised for the Isle of Rhé expedition in 1627, these had 12 companies each, each company comprising 83 soldiers plus their captain, lieutenant and ensign.[31]

On 29 July 1629 a regiment commanded by Sir Charles Morgan was being readied to serve in the Low Countries.[32] The men had originally been formed into two regiments, but due to a decrease in the number of soldiers there was now only one. Originally 20 companies had been available, four of these were in the Channel Islands and another four had been disbanded with the men being sent to other companies. The regiment was to be 16 companies strong, including those in the Channel Islands, and the order for this regiment also

27 John R. Dasent (ed.), *Acts of the Privy Council of England, Volume 39, 1623–1625* (London: HMSO, 1933), pp.385–6.

28 J.V. Lyle (ed.), *Acts of the Privy Council of England*, Volume 40, 1625–1626 (London: HMSO, 1934), pp.141–2

29 Lyle, *Acts of the Privy Council of England, 1625–1626*, pp.325–7.

30 J.V. Lyle, *Acts of the Privy Council of England*, New Series, Volume 41, January–August 1627 (London: HMSO, 1938), pp.187–190.

31 J.V. Lyle, *Acts of the Privy Council of England*, New Series, Volume 42, 1627 September–1628 June (London: HMSO, 1940 (London: HMSO, 1940), pp.15–16.

32 John R. Dasent, *Acts of the Privy Council of England*, New Series, Volume 45, 1629 May–1630 May (London, HMSO, 1960), p.109.

included their pay for 42 days. The strength of the companies in the regiment varied depending on the rank of the commander: the colonel's company was 200 men strong, the lieutenant colonel's and sergeant major's companies 150 strong and the captain's companies 115 men strong. The pay for 42 days for this regiment was to be as follows:

> Colonel, 525 guilders
> Lieutenant colonel, 131½ guilders
> Sergeant major, 105 guilders
> Quartermaster, 105 guilders
> Provost, 65 guilders
> Surgeon, 50 guilders
> Preacher, 23½ guilders
> Paymaster, £150 per annum and the 100th penny
> Soldiers, 13–14 guilders

In 1631 the King had agreed to send 6,000 volunteers from England and Wales to serve in the Swedish Army. These men were organised into three foot regiments, each regiment comprising 10 companies, a colonel's company, a lieutenant colonel's company, a sergeant major's company and seven captain's companies. Theoretically each regiment should have numbered 2,000 men, but warrants issued on 8 June 1631 give each company a strength of 150 men, an overall total of 4,500 men for the three regiments.[33]

The Trained Band Regiments

Having already touched upon the regimental organisations more details will now be provided. The counties of Somerset and Wiltshire and the city of Bristol had the same lord lieutenant, and both of the counties raised regiments, but the counties had differing organisations. Somerset had four foot regiments, each of 800 men organised into six captain's companies of 100 men and a colonel's company of 200 men. Wiltshire also had four foot regiments but these numbered 600 men each, comprising four captain's companies of 100 men and a colonel's company of 200 men. Bristol had three companies of 100 men each, but no regiment.

Between 1633 and 1639 the Yorkshire Trained Band foot was organised into 14 regiments of foot, these being grouped by the Riding they were raised in. The East Riding provided four regiments numbering 3,440 men; the North Riding also provided four regiments totalling 4,000 men, and the West Riding, six regiments totalling 4,800 men.[34] The references to regimental strengths are noted in the sections below.

Information on the regimental organisation for the Yorkshire regiments is fragmentary. There is information on the organisation of the county's foot

---

33 John R. Dasent, *Acts of the Privy Council of England*, New Series, Volume 46, 1630–1631 (London: HMSO, 1964), pp.376–8.

34 British Library Add MS 36913, and British Library Add MS 28082, ff.80–81.

regiments in the British Library document Add MS 28082 for the period 1633–35. This document shows that the regiments varied in strength and organisation, the size of the regiments varying from 600 to 1,300 men and the number of companies from five to 10. There is additional information on three of the regiments in the West Riding in 1638 in the West Yorkshire Archives.[35] There are also a number of documents available which provide details on a number of company organisations. In 1613 Sir William Constable's company was 200 strong, in 1615 the trained band of Richmondshire had a strength of 200 men, in 1625 Sir John Buck's company had 125 men, and the 1626 muster roll for Sir John Ramsden's company gives a strength of 150 men while Sir John Reresby's company numbered 110 men in 1633.[36]

Whilst the company strengths do not help with the Yorkshire regimental organisation, the information from the 1633–35 document does give an important clue by including the number of companies and the strength of each regiment. As we have seen, there does not appear to be a standardised company strength, see Table 7.

Table 7. Organisation of Yorkshire foot regiments 1633–35

Riding	Regiment	Nr of Coys	Nr of Men
West	Ramsden, Sir John	5	600
West	Stanhope, Sir Edward	5	600
East	Constable, Sir William	6	800
East	Boynton, Sir Matthew	6	800
East	Griffith, Sir Henry	6	800
North	Hoby, Sir Thomas	6	800
West	Mallory, William, Mr	6	800
West	Savile, Sir William	6	800
North	Fairfax, Lord Viscount	7	900
North	Penniman, Sir William	5	1,000
West	Rodes, Sir Edward	8	1,000
West	Ramsden, Sir John	5	600
West	Stanhope, Sir Edward	5	600

There are six regiments with 800 men and six companies, one regiment of 900 with seven companies and two regiments with 1,000 men and eight companies. These figures indicate that if equally distributed then each captain's company contained 100 men. If we subtract the totals for the captain's companies from each of the regimental totals we have 300 men left, this could indicate the colonel's company being 300 strong, a figure not seen in any of the returns. Looking at some of the other regimental

35 West Yorkshire Archives Service, 32D86/38, f.257.
36 British Library, Add Ch 54396.

organisations used, these 300 men could indicate a colonel's company of 200, a lieutenant colonel's company of 160 and the sergeant major's company of 140 men. This was an organisation that was used at the start of the Civil War. Having said this, not all the regiments fit this pattern which shows that most counties, like Yorkshire, did not have a uniform organisation for their trained band units.

During the early years of his reign Charles had invested time and money in the development of the "exact militia", and by 1639, the year of the 1st Bishops' War, many county trained bands had reached a competent level of training. There were problems with them, however: one of these was their unwillingness to serve outside of their home county. Many of the men were farmers or businessmen who could not afford to be away from their trade for any length of time. The other, long-term problem was the horse troops.

This reluctance to serve away from home and business led to the use of pressed men to take the place of the trained bands in foreign expeditions, and also led to the introduction of the "substitution clause" by Charles for the 2nd Bishops' War. This clause allowed a member of the trained band to pay someone else to take his place in the ranks to fight against the Scots. There were many problems with this compromise: the men were untrained, not equipped with serviceable weapons and many were not motivated to fight for King and country. Some of these pressed men were the undesirables from the various localities, the war being an ideal opportunity to get rid of them. Another issue was that membership of the trained band usually exempted men from being pressed for these foreign expeditions.[37]

Fighting in the two Bishops' Wars against the Presbyterians in Scotland, and against the Catholic revolt in Ireland, were not what the trained bands were intended for and yet they were all that was readily available. The war in Ireland did not immediately impact directly on the counties of England and Wales, however the wars against the Scots did. Men from the counties were sent north to fight against the Scots in the Bishops' Wars, mostly untrained, pressed men. It did not go well for them.

We have a good idea of the strength of the trained bands for the counties of England and Wales thanks to the preparations of Charles I for the two Bishops' Wars: Charles needed to know the numbers of men he theoretically had available to him and how they were equipped. A full survey of the numbers and types of soldiers was made in 1638;[38] the totals for England and Wales are given as 54,517 musketeers, 39,081 pikemen and 5,239 horsemen.

We do know that the county trained band regiments destined for Scotland in 1638 were to have had a theoretical strength of 1,000 men and that Charles wanted this to be increased to 1,500 men.[39] On 18 December 1638 he ordered Sir Jacob Astley to look into this, and on 19 December he repeated this order to the lord lieutenants of the counties

---

37 Lyle, *Acts of the Privy Council of England*, 1625–1626, p.172.
38 The National Archives, SP16/381.
39 Calendar of State Papers, Domestic Series, volume CCCCIV.

of Staffordshire, Cheshire, Lancashire, Nottinghamshire, Leicestershire and Rutland, Lincoln and Derby. Despite this order to Astley we know from the returns of 1640 for the army in the north that the standard paper strength for the regiments was 1,200 men, although some were stronger or weaker.[40] Although these men were pressed for service and not the trained bands, the regimental organisation, being contemporary, is still worth looking at. Those regiments with a theoretical strength of 1,200 men had 10 companies: the colonel's company of 200 men, the lieutenant colonel's company with 160 men, the sergeant major's company with 140 men and the seven captain's companies each with 100 men. In February 1642, with war now becoming imminent, the City of London's trained bands were increased to a strength of 40 companies with each company being 200 men strong.[41] These companies were used to form six new regiments, the four old ones being disbanded, four of the regiments had seven companies, the Red, White, Yellow and Blue, while the remaining two, the Green and Orange, had six companies each.

The organisation of the horse is a little more difficult to work out on a county basis. The first problem is that in 1640 cavalry was classed as lancer, light, cuirassier, harquebusier or dragoon. The number and type of horse being raised also varied county by county, so it would seem unlikely that there was a standard organisation within the county although these were often referred to as companies.

Tactical Organisation

Evidence of the actual tactics and formations employed by the trained band is not easily found, although a number of documents containing tactical organisation information do exist, dating from 1616 to 1640.

A handwritten document from Norfolk from the 1620s comprises four unnumbered pieces of paper, each containing the names of the men forming either a division of pikes or muskets. Overall the document shows a company

Tables 8–11. A division of pikes or muskets, Norfolk, 1620s

L/hand ranks	Files, Pikes, 1 Division				Files r/hand
	5 pikes	5pikes	5 pikes	5 pikes	5 pikes
Middle men	3 pikes	5 pikes	5 pikes	5 pikes	5 pikes

L/hand ranks	Files, Pikes, 2 Division Front				Files r/hand
	blank	5 pikes	5 pikes	5 pikes	5 pikes
		4 pikes	5 pikes	5 pikes	4 pikes
		Rear			

---

40   S.F. Jones (ed.), *English Army Lists of the Early 1640s* (Reading: Tyger's Head Books, 2015).

41   Wilfrid Emberton, *Skippon's Brave Boys: the origins, development and Civil War service of the London trained Bands* (London: Barracuda Books Ltd, 1984), p.61.

L/hand ranks	Files musketeers				Files r/hand
Half files	5 muskets All names crossed out	5 musk.	5 musk.	5 musk.	5 muskets
Middle men	3 muskets All names crossed out	5 musk.	5 musk.	5 musk.	5 muskets
L/hand ranks	Files musket 2nd division				Files r/hand
	5 muskets	5 musk.	5 musk.	5 musk.	5 musk.
	5 muskets	5 musk.	5 musk.	5 musk.	5 musk.
Rear					

organised into two divisions, each comprising muskets and pikes.[42] The pikes and muskets of each division are shown as files and ranks as per Tables 8–11.

Other Categories

In 1619 the Dorset Trained Band was reported to have 100 horse and 3,429 foot.[43] Following the 1628 musters the deputies reported the current state of the county's forces to the Lord Lieutenant.[44] Firstly, the Isle of Purbeck refused to muster with the rest of the county, so its foot companies were not included in their return. Secondly, the deputies reported that they had included the troop bands with the trained bands. The troop bands were only mustered twice a year, much of the arms and armour was obsolete calivers and curats, and these were provided by men of lesser means, usually grouped three or four together to pay for a musket or a corslet or equivalent. These men had been formed into seven companies of 100 men each. Thirdly, besides the trained band and the troop bands there was a third category, men selected to defend the castles and other points on the coast which were open to attack. There were more than 200 men in this unnamed category. Lastly, the deputies noted that the forts of Brancksey (now Brownsea), Portland and Sandsfoot lacked ammunition and carriages. In November 1629 the Lord Lieutenant reported to the Privy Council that at the last muster the county fielded 100 horse and 2,350 foot, comprising 1,010 pikemen and 1,340 musketeers.[45] This was a loss of over 1,000 men in 10 years. In a later report in October 1635, the Lord Lieutenant reported to the Privy Council that at the musters just held the trained band numbered 100 horse and 1,500 foot, another drop. He also reported that the other forces in the county, called troop bands, did not usually muster and were ill-armed, but numbered some 1,580 men. He wanted 600 of these to be

---

42 Norfolk Record Office, NAS 1/1/2/15.
43 Bodleian Library MS Firth c4.
44 The National Archives, SP 16/120, f.8.
45 The National Archives, SP 16/151, f.86.

taken into the trained band to make the numbers up to 2,100, and form these men into three regiments, presumably with 700 in each. He awaited the Privy Council's approval.[46] These plans were apparently approved because in February 1638 the trained band was reported as having 100 horse and 2,140 foot, comprising 1,444 musketeers and 696 pikemen.[47]

---

46 17 Oct 1635, Suffolk House, Calendar of State Papers, Domestic, Vol. CCXCIX, p.434.
47 Calendar of State Papers, Domestic, February 1638.

Cast about y^r Musket

Hould your Musket in both hands as before
beare it right up towards your left side
and with all step forwards the right leg
then holding the Musket only in the right
hand at the breast forsake the rest.

3

The Officers and the Soldiers in the Trained Bands

The Officers

If a county had formed one or more foot regiments there was a colonel, a lieutenant colonel and a sergeant major for each regiment, regardless of the number of companies in the regiment. The colonel was often, but not always, a deputy lieutenant. All three of these ranks would also have had a company under their command, and as far as this company was concerned, they were the captain. This means that they had a company rank of captain and a regimental rank with both ranks being used interchangeably.

The captains in charge of the individual foot companies were chosen by the lord lieutenant of their county, or in some cases by the deputy lieutenants, but these would need to be confirmed by the lord lieutenant. If the lord lieutenant was not resident in the county but wanted to choose the captains he would normally ask his deputies for a list of men they considered to be suitable; this usually happened when the lord lieutenant was not resident in the county and trusted the deputies to make the right choice. Many of the captains already held positions of responsibility within their county, serving as Members of Parliament and Justices of the Peace. The captain would usually live in the recruiting area of the company that he was to command. On being appointed he would be given his commission informing him what was expected of him. A number of examples of these commissions can be found in Appendix I. Each company would also have a lieutenant, an ensign or ancient, and sometimes a clerk as well as a number of what we would nowadays call non-commissioned officers. The sergeants, who were counted as officers, were also appointed by the captain and were usually men who had served in the ranks of the trained band for a number of years and usually promoted from corporal. It was not unusual for the sergeants to become ensigns or lieutenants within their company. Below the sergeants were the corporals and lansprisados, but these will be discussed later.

The company officers seem to have been selected by the captain. This implies a personal connection, often a family connection, a brother or son being selected to be the company's lieutenant or ensign. Between 1629 and 1633 in Devon, many of the officers in the foot companies appear to have had family connections;[1] out of 40 foot companies at least eight had a direct family connection. In Hampshire the same surname occurred a number of times within the ranks of the officers. In some counties men were employed who were known within their communities and could command respect within them. In Leicestershire in 1640 the lieutenant in Colonel Sir Thomas Brooke's Company was Robert Willsheire.[2] He was a draper from Market Harborough, the main town in the company's recruiting area, and presumably known by many people in the town and the company.

There were occasions when dissenting voices were raised following some trained band appointments. In 1604 Sir William Jopson or Jephson of Froyle (1565–1615) was noted as the captain of a foot company in Hampshire. Sir William's appointment coincides with his election as an MP in 1604, however his constituents tried to have him removed on the grounds that he was blind.[3] If this were true then his service as a trained band captain would have been difficult.

There were other incidents involving trained band officers, Sir William Withipole of Sudborne, Suffolk, being one. He was elected to Parliament in 1625 and had been appointed as a deputy lieutenant in 1623, serving until at least 1626. He was also a captain in the trained band foot by 1627, attaining the rank of colonel in 1628, and served until at least 1632 when he was obliged to go abroad. He was pardoned in 1643 but took no part in the Civil War.[4] Whatever his faults he evidently inspired loyalty in his men. In 1628 he became involved in a dispute between one of his brothers, who was accused of being a Catholic by a Suffolk clergyman called John Rous, and an officer named Maddison. Matters came to a head in late June 1628 when Sir William marched his company out of Ipswich and encountered Maddison and his soldiers on Martlesham Heath, about six miles to the east of Ipswich. According to John Rous, Sir William Withipole and his brother "did cowardly pistol" Maddison and another man; this was followed by an exchange of shots between the two companies resulting in one death, a man who was accidentally shot by another man who was stood behind him. Sir William reportedly marched his men back to Ipswich, where he had the church bells rung, and the following day he went to London to exonerate himself. Instead, he was committed to stand trial in King's Bench for murder.

It was generally thought that Sir William Withipole was guilty. The trial does not seem to have taken place until the following April, when Withipole and his co-defendants were all acquitted of murder, but found guilty of manslaughter. The 1st Earl of Berkshire (Sir Thomas Howard), who had presumably become acquainted with Sir William when they were both serving Charles when he was the Prince of Wales, procured a pardon for Withipole, undertaking that the latter would abide by any order made for satisfaction of the relatives of his

---

1   The National Archives, SP 16/70, f.22, and SP 16/150, f.112.
2   Leicestershire Record Office, DG5/900/4.
3   <http://www.historyofparliamentonline.org/volume/1604-1629/member/jephson-sir-william-1565-1615>, accessed 6 September 2020.
4   <http://www.historyofparliamentonline.org/volume/1604-1629/member/withypoll-sir-william-1596-1645>, accessed 16 March 2017.

victims. Apparently the King was unhappy that Withipole had got away so lightly, and ordered that the jury be arraigned in the Star Chamber.

The Foot Soldiers

There were two main categories of soldier in the foot companies of the trained bands, private and common. The private soldier was paid for by one or more individual person, man or woman, adult or child in the case of an heir or heiress, dead or alive. The charge on them would be for the purchase, as and when needed, of the soldier's equipment, its maintenance or replacement, the pay of the soldier and his expenses in the field. When a group of people were brought together to maintain a soldier, it might be that they paid an agreed amount each and the total was used for those purposes. Sometimes each individual would be responsible for buying and maintaining a particular piece of the soldier's equipment or his training expenses. Additionally, the soldier might himself be one of the people paying for the equipment he was using or serving himself at his own charge. The soldiers provided by the clergy fall into this private category although the clergymen themselves would never have served in the ranks of the trained bands. The common soldiers were so called because of the fact that the community, the town or village where they lived, paid for them and their equipment and not because they themselves were common.

A good example of these arrangements is recorded in the muster book for South Molton in Devon for the year 1632.[5] A few examples are shown in Table 12.

Table 12. Furnishing arrangements, South Molton, 1632

Village	Soldier's forename	Soldier's surname	Arm	Private/ Common	Furnished by
Chittlehampton	Baldwin	Acland	Corslet	Private	Himself
Chittlehampton	John	Drew	Corslet	Private	Arthur Sander, John Cawsey & Henry Megford the corslet & pike, James Ley the sword & belt
Chittlehampton	John	Dorracott	Musket	Private	His father, the musket & bandaleer, John Cawsey, the sword & belt & John Foard, the headpiece, bag & mold
Chittlehampton	William	Cawsey	Musket	Private	Mistress Anne Acland, widow
Chittlehampton	Thomas	Lymebeare	Musket	Private	His mother
Swimbridge	John	Ridgway	Corslet	Private	Himself and Widow Maire, with the whole jointly

---

5   Devon Heritage Centre, Z19/46/7.

One issue that could and did occur was the question of who was responsible for the arms and armour when it was being used and when it was not being used. It would seem that the owner of the arms and armour stored what belonged to them at home, and this is borne out by a number of Cheshire inventories taken when people had died. When Edward Baskerfield of Sound died in 1613 the corslet he owned was valued at 26s 8d, it would appear that this was left to his wife Elizabeth, as when she died in 1617 the value of the corslet had decreased to 20s. Roger Hockenhull of Broomhall, gentleman, who died in 1614, had his corslet, furnished, and his plate coat valued at £5; this indicated that the corslet, furnished, probably included the helmet, sword and pike. In 1616 when Thomas Gray of Smeatonwood died, he had a musket valued at 20s, and yet in 1624 when George Cudworth of Newhall, gentleman, died he left a musket with furniture, his family's armour, a crossbow, a stonebow, other artillery, two swords and a stave, all valued at 20s. In Charles' reign the same items come up in wills and inventories quite regularly. When John Cartwright junior of Aston, gentleman, died in 1630, he had a corslet with its furniture, this was valued at £2 10s, again this would have included his helmet, sword and the pike. John Bromehall of Sound also died in 1630, he left a quantity of equipment comprising two muskets, one fowling piece, two pairs of bandoleers, one cap, one sword, two girdles, powder and shot, all valued at a mere £2 13s 4d. The inventory for John Cartwright of Sheppenhall, Aston, gentleman, taken in November 1631, lists one musket with furniture, this would be the musket rest, bullet bag, bullet mould and so on, valued at only 15s. Another John Cartwright, gentleman, of the same place, had a fowling piece, a musket, a headpiece and some bandoleers valued at £1 11s in his inventory in January 1635. The last firearm mentioned was in the inventory of George Tench of Smeatonwood in 1638, his two swords and a musket were valued at only 10s. Finally the inventory of Thomas Gray of Newhall, yeoman, taken in March 1640, listed artillery valued at £1 3s 4d[6].

Problems could occur when arms and armour were being used at musters for training. If they were damaged, who paid for repair or replacement? In Ludlow in 1625 William Doggerell, a musketeer, damaged his musket during training, this was then declared defective and needed to be replaced.[7] The cost of the arms and armour and training provided to William Doggerell was paid for by a group of three men. One of these, Thomas Watkins, a mercer, paid for the arms and armour while the other two men paid for the training. Watkins wanted the new musket to be paid for by Doggerell, despite the latter being described as being a poor man with no money. Watkins initiated a court action, which he won and then set the debt collectors onto Doggerell who in turn petitioned the Lord Lieutenant to have the case quashed. In the meantime the two men responsible for providing Doggerell's training costs had bought a new musket themselves at no cost to Watkins, who it would seem was determined to have Doggerell put in gaol. The Lord Lieutenant

---

6   Paul B. Pixton (ed.), Wrenbury wills and inventories 1542–1661 (Chester: The Record Society of Lancashire and Cheshire, 2009), pp,117, 126, 127, 154, 157, 158, 199, 200, 251, 272, 295, 329, 347.
7   Shropshire Archives, LB14/871.

summoned the town's bailiffs to come and speak with him at Ludlow Castle, hoping to find a way that satisfied both men. This must have worked out amicably as Doggerell continued as a soldier for another year with the same group of maintainers.

Having mentioned the clergy, their involvement was always an uneasy matter. Their integration into the county military infrastructure, especially in the first quarter of the seventeenth century, was difficult. In some counties the men they provided were integrated into the foot companies, although in at least one county there was a separate company for them. The decision of what the clergy should provide was decided by the Bishop in charge of the diocese, following instructions from either of the Archbishops of Canterbury or York.

Soldiers Raised by Officeholders and Trade Guilds

The city of Worcester raised its soldiers by a fairly simple method, agreed upon at a meeting held on 14 July 1615.[8] The aldermen, referred to as the "24", were required to provide arms and armour for a pikeman each, while 48 other men were required to provide the arms and armour for a musketeer each. In addition the Bailiff was tasked with identifying and charging the city's wealthier citizens with providing arms and armour appropriate to their "estate and ability". Should anyone fail to provide the arms and armour they were charged with, they were to be fined at a set rate. Any member of the "24" was to be fined 10s, the "48", 6s 8d and any commoner, 5s. This requirement was repeated on 18 June 1635 and again on 14 September 1638. On the latter occasion, the fines for failing to do so were increased. Now any member of the "24" defaulting was to be fined 20s, the "48", 10s and any commoner, 6s 8d. On 17 March 1626 Worcester Corporation carried out a survey of all the arms held within the city with the additional aim of finding more of its citizens who were able to provide arms and armour. Another source of these were the trade guilds or companies, who were also required to furnish arms and armour.

The towns of Ludlow and Shrewsbury in Shropshire had two different systems for providing their trained soldiers. Ludlow used a system whereby the wealthier people in the town paid for their 24 soldiers' equipment and wages either individually or as a group. These people were termed as finders and maintainers and were obliged to attend the musters along with the soldiers they paid for. Shrewsbury's method entailed their 39 soldiers being funded by either the various trade guilds or the parishes within the town and liberty of Shrewsbury.[9]

The use of the categories of "private" and "common" soldiers is important, as is the use of the terms "selected" and "unselected", and "trained" and "untrained". The "private" and "common" categories have already been covered, and the rest will now be discussed. The descriptions "selected" and

---

8   Shelagh Bond (ed.), *The Chamber Order Book of Worcester, 1602–50*, WHS volume 8 (Worcester: Worcestershire Historical Society, 1974), pp.132–133, 203–4.

9   Shropshire Archives, 3365/2563/1–6.

"unselected" come from the practice of some counties of training slightly more men that they needed and then selecting the best of those who had been trained; Northamptonshire used this system, while other counties simply selected the number of men required and trained them, such as the Cinque Ports did. The muster lists from Northamptonshire for the East and West Divisions show this selection process. For the East Division the muster returns for the years 1605 and 1613–19 have been used. In 1605, 320 men were trained, 20 more than needed. For the period between 1613 and 1619 the returns for only half of the Division are available. The totals of trained men for this period varied between 160 and 179 men, and these figures give a surplus of between 10 and 19 trained men per year. The muster returns for the years 1632, 1634 and 1635 for the West Division have been used and give totals of trained soldiers of 396, 392 and 352 respectively.[10] Both divisions only had to supply 300 trained soldiers each. These 300 soldiers were classed as trained and selected with the remainder being trained but unselected. At the end of the musters the actual men selected varied from year to year.

In a letter to the Privy Council dated 16 October 1615, the Nottinghamshire commissioners for musters referred to the trained band as the "Trained or Common Band".[11] This implies that in this county the trained band did not contain any private soldiers.

Besides the trained soldiers there were also substantial numbers of untrained men. Some counties organised them and gave some training to these men on a similar basis to the trained soldiers, and in Lancashire they were organised into regiments and companies as previously discussed. There were musters of the untrained men as ordered by the Privy Council, usually all able-bodied men aged 16 to 60 being required to attend a muster and be assessed, physically, for their suitability to serve. The numbers of these men can be seen from Table 13.

Another category of soldiers was the pioneers. These men were not armed with a pike or a musket but could have a bill for their defence; they were equipped with various tools, spades, picks, axes, etc. and were responsible for any field engineering that was required. A ratio of 10 pioneers per 100 trained soldiers was recommended by the Privy Council.

What sort of men served in the trained band? The Privy Council issued instructions on a number of occasions giving the requirements for being a trained band soldier. The trained band was intended to be composed of men who were well-affected in religion – in other words Protestant – were reasonably prosperous, able bodied and had a stake in the community. The officers and the men were required to take the Oath of Supremacy and Oath of Allegiance as part of their training (see Appendix VIII). Men serving in the trained band were excluded from being chosen as village constables, another duty many wanted to avoid.[12] It also had the advantage of making that man

---

10   Northamptonshire record Office, CA7506, Cartwright Muster Book.

11   The National Archives, SP 14/82, f.68.

12   H. Hampton Copnall and Henry B. Saxton, *Nottinghamshire County Records. Notes & extracts from the Nottinghamshire county records of the 17th century* (Nottingham: H.B. Saxton, 1915), p.18.

Table 13. Numbers of untrained men mustered, 1629–1631

County/Town	Number	Year
Anglesey	800	1629
Berkshire, Reading	1,098	1626
Brecon	6,138	1608
Buckinghamshire	4,532	1620
Cheshire	7,408	1636
Derbyshire	17,411	1638
Derbyshire	17,308	1639
Devon, Exeter	919	1638
Devon, Hundred of Coleridge	899	1619
Devon, Hundred of Stanborough	525	1619
Devon, less Exeter & the Tinners	6,745	1633
Durham	11,092	1635
Glamorgan	1,400	1631
Glamorgan	1,400	1635
Gloucester liberties	1,379	1635
Gloucester town	980	1635
Kent	21,513	1635
Kent	20,276	1639
Lancashire	7,408	1636
Lancashire, Manchester	1,456	1626
Lincolnshire	15,000	1635
Middlesex	25,000	1636
Staffordshire	6,000	1627
Suffolk	10,527	1615
Suffolk, Bury St Edmunds	1,335	1635
Surrey	3,711	1627–38
Wiltshire	20,000	1635
Yorkshire	87,689	1635

exempt from being pressed for overseas service, until Charles I tried to press the trained bands for his wars against the Scots. Oddly, it was not stated that a man had to be English or Welsh and there are examples of foreigners serving in the trained bands. In Norwich two of the five companies were comprised entirely of foreigners, one company of Walloons and the other of Dutchmen, including the noted military author, John Cruso, who served as their captain. In 1640 Cruso was acting as an agent in Norfolk for Philip Skippon, then residing in London.[13] Skippon was to become famous as the commander of the London Trained Bands in the Civil War. In the Sandwich Trained Band there were also a number of Dutchmen serving as musketeers in its ranks in 1638.

On 23 June 1617, Lord Gerard, the lord lieutenant, wrote to Sir Robert Needham and Sir Robert Vernon.[14] He noted that he wanted none but "choice and selected men of worth and quality to serve in the Trained Band". These were men who were going to have an interest in a stable community.

The physical fitness of the soldiers was important to the authorities. On 20 March 1627 the deputy lieutenants in Norfolk wrote to the chief constables of the county's hundreds,[15] wanting them to encourage manly and warlike physical activities such as archery, running, wrestling, leaping, football, throwing the hammer and playing at cudgels. They wanted these activities to replace what they saw as the current ones engaged in by the local men, namely drinking and spending leisure time in the ale houses.

In 1608 a document was produced for the county of Gloucester, which listed all the able-bodied men in the county.[16] In many cases their age group and their trade were included. The majority of those who were members of the trained band were also noted. A total of 2,046 men were identified as being soldiers in the trained band; the county actually provided a force of 3,000 foot, but enough were identified to give us a good picture of the men who served in 1608.

A total of 1,597 members of the Gloucestershire trained band soldiers were noted with their trades, which were very varied. The most common were the husbandmen, 46.3 percent, the next group were the yeomen, 12.6 percent, followed by the weavers, 8.3 percent. There were a number of unusual trades noted with only one man practising each; these included an apothecary, a horse-rider, a shipwright and a goldsmith.

Of interest is the inclusion of information on the stature of all the Gloucestershire men. These fall into four categories: "the tallest stature fit to be a pikeman", "a middle stature fit to make a musketeer", "a lower stature fit to serve with a caliver" and "the meanest stature either fit for a pioneer or of little use".

The age groups of the Gloucestershire men were also recorded, these were "about 20", "about forty" and "between 50 and 3 score", the present author has

---

13   British Library Egerton MS 2716, f.360.

14   Historical Manuscripts Commission, *Tenth Report*, p.365.

15   Rye, *State papers relating to musters*, pp.60–61.

16   John Smith (ed.), *Men & Armour for Gloucestershire in 1608* (Gloucester: Alan Sutton Publishing Ltd, 1980).

taken these groups to be up to 29, 30 to 49 and 50 to 60 years old, for reasons which will become clear when information from other counties is looked at. Of the 1,754 men whose age group was given, 19.6 percent were aged up to 29, the 30 to 49-year-old group comprised 73.8 percent and those aged between 50 and 60 totalled 6.6 percent. The allocation of weapons against the age groups is of interest, remembering the description of the physical stature of the men, Table 14 contains this information, 1,748 men were noted with their age and weapon.

Table 14. Ratios of arms, Somerset 1608

Ratios of arms			Ratios of arms by age		
Weapon	Totals	Percentages	=>29 years of age	30–49 years of age	50–60 years of age
Pike	680	39.4%	36.3%	39.3%	50.0%
Musket	589	33.7%	32.0%	34.4%	30.7%
Caliver	470	26.9%	31.7%	26.3%	19.3%
Totals	1,748	100%	100%	100%	100%

There is also similar information for the Leicestershire Trained Band for 1638 and 1640.[17] Of the 138 men whose ages could be determined the youngest was 18 years old and the oldest was 50. The overall average age was 32, with the average pikeman aged 32 and the average musketeer 34. The overall figures for Leicestershire are given in Table 15. Of the 138 men whose age group can be ascertained, 42.0 percent were aged up to 29, the 30- to 49-year-old group comprised 57.2 percent and those aged 50 to 60 totalled 0.7 percent. A comparison of the percentages for weapon type against the age groups shows that the younger men were more likely to be pikemen and the older men more likely to be musketeers.

Table 15. Numbers of arms, Leicestershire 1638–40

Numbers of arms		Numbers of men by arms and age		
Weapon	Totals	=>29 years of age	30–49 years of age	50–60 years of age
Pike	58	30	28	0
Musket	80	28	51	1
Totals	138	58	79	1

---

17   Leicestershire Record Office, DG5/895-911.

The muster records for the town of Ludlow in Shropshire are also of note. The town provided only 24 trained soldiers per year, and the records cover the years from 1624 to 1640. The average age of the soldiers when they joined the trained band was 29, and 37 when they were last noted in the ranks.[18] The soldiers were equally divided between pikes and muskets, so a comparison of such a small group is not really worthwhile statistically speaking.

An analysis of one of the foot companies in Hertfordshire in 1634, Sir John Luke's Company, gives an interesting insight into the soldiers' ages from that county.[19] The company is made up of 307 soldiers, private and common, pikemen (corslets) and musketeers, exclusive of the supernumeraries. Table 16 contains this data.

Table 16. Sir John Luke's Company, Hertfordshire 1634

	Private (nr)	Common (nr)	Totals (nr)	Private (%)	Common (%)	Totals (%)
Corslets	109	25	134	81.3%	18.7%	43.6%
Muskets	149	24	173	86.1%	13.9%	56.4%
Totals	258	49	307	84.0%	16.0%	

The ages of the men serving as soldiers is also of interest. Of the 624 men, the ages of 176 of them can be determined, the youngest being aged 18 and the oldest 50. The average age for the soldiers, overall, was 32 with the average for the musketeers being 31 and the pikemen 33. The divide between the private and common and pikemen and musketeers was also of note, see Table 17.

Table 17. Sir John Luke's Company, Hertfordshire 1634

	Nr of years attending musters	Nr of soldiers attending the musters	Percentages of soldiers attending the musters
For one year	1	37	18.5%
For two years	2	26	13.0%
For three years	3	27	13.5%
For four years	4	110	55.0%
Total		200	100%

---

18 Shropshire Archives, LB/2181/1–21.
19 Folger Shakespeare Library, Washington DC, va576.

Two muster returns for Derbyshire, those for 1621 and 1639, give the names of the soldiers. A study of these returns shows possible family connections between them. The list for 1621 does not cover the entire county, only three of the wapentakes are included,[20] while the list for 1639 covers the whole county.[21] This does enable a comparison to be made of the soldiers from those three wapentakes. Of the 90 soldiers from Scarsdale Wapentake, the names of 16 of them appeared in both lists, from the same towns and villages. This could mean that they had served for at least 18 years or that they were related, possibly father and son. Another 13 surnames appeared on both lists, from the same villages, and a check on the baptism records indicates that some of these were probably father and son. In both scenarios the men carried the same type of weapon in 1621 and 1639. The figures for the same criteria for the High Peak Wapentake are 80 men, 22 with the same name and 15 with the same surname, again all from the same village or town with the same weapon type. Wirkesworth Wapentake only had 50 men and oddly had much lower numbers, just two men with the same name and four with the same surname, again from the same villages and towns with the same weapon types.

The Horse

The trained band horse was entirely private, paid for by wealthy individuals or groups of better-off people including the clergy. There is very little information on the men who served as horsemen. There are a number of complaints raised about the riders only meeting the horses at the musters, sometimes for the first and last time. Their ability to actually ride seems to have been of little interest to the owners of the horses who, not unnaturally for them, were more concerned about their property than the man assigned to ride it.

---

20 Derby Local Studies and Family History Library, Kerry, vol. 19, pp.85–130, transcript of document at Belvoir Castle; The National Archives, SP 14/78, f.74.
21 Derbyshire Record Office, D156/MO/21.

Trayle y^r Rest

JO

Having forsaken y^r rest take y^e Musket into
y^e left hand about y^e midle of y^e barrell soe
as y^e butt end touch not the ground trayling
your rest betweene y^e Musket and bodie

4

The Musters

Musters were called at a number of levels usually for one of two purposes: viewing the men and their equipment to check for defects in either, or viewing the men and their equipment and then training the men in the equipment's use, and then following the training, exercising them.

General musters were supposed to be called once per year in every county, usually in response to an order from the King via the Privy Council. These took place in most if not all of the counties and often included the able-bodied men aged between 16 and 60 who were not members of the trained band. These usually involved all the soldiers within the county, either together or in smaller groups at convenient places, preferably on the same day. Events did take place which sometimes forced the suspension of these musters, for example, heavy rain or snow could stop, delay or prevent training being carried out. However, the main reason for a postponement or even a cancellation of the musters was an outbreak of the plague, also referred to as "the sickness".

Under the statutes of Philip and Mary, the men provided by the clergy were permitted to be mustered separately from those mustered by the laity. Needless to say, the clergy were not enthusiastic about attending the musters or sending the arms and armour that they were charged with.

In September 1608 concerns about the levels of plague infection in Surrey, especially around Southwark, led to concerns about holding the musters.[1] The Lord Lieutenant informed his deputies of his concerns and intended to ask for a deferment, and on 9 October 1608 wrote to the Privy Council asking for the musters to be delayed.[2] On 12 October he wrote to his four current deputies – his son, Lord William Howard, Sir Francis Carew, Sir George More and Sir Thomas Vincent[3] – and confirmed the deferment of the county muster until the plague had subsided. He also told them that the muster would be for the trained band only and not a general muster. The Privy Council replied to the Lord Lieutenant on 16 October to tell him that

---

1   Surrey History Centre, 6729/9/77.
2   Mary Anne Everett Green (ed.), *Calendar of State Papers, Domestic Series, of the Reign of James I, 1603–10* (London: Longman, Brown, Green, Longmans, & Roberts, 1857), p.461.
3   Surrey History Centre, 6729/4/126.

due to the outbreak of the plague Surrey's muster could be postponed until it was safe to hold it.[4]

Two of the lord lieutenants of Sussex wrote to the deputies on 11 March 1609 regarding holding a muster and view of the trained band.[5] They were aware of the presence of "the sickness" in the county but believed it to be decreasing. They wanted to know whether the deputies thought it would be safe to hold musters without causing another outbreak.

On 30 October 1614 the Lord Lieutenant of Derbyshire informed the Privy Council that Sir Peter Frecheville and Sir John Harpur, two of the deputy lieutenants, had written to him on 20 October to tell him that the county musters had been held. The men had been trained and exercised as well as they could, but allowances for the wet weather had had to be made.[6] In Derbyshire in 1621 the weather was so wet that the musters were not held that year.

Sometimes musters were held but the muster certificate was not sent in. The Privy Council wrote to the three lord lieutenants of Sussex on 30 April 1616.[7] They began by complaining about other counties that had not sent in their muster certificates, which they presumed was because of the poor state of the trained bands in those counties. This is not the only instance of this happening. The view of the counties themselves was probably something along the lines of "if we don't tell the Privy Council things are bad they won't know. If they don't know we can't be at fault."

Viewing

The purpose of a viewing was quite simple. Firstly to ensure that the men were alive and physically fit for service – this was after all an era when death could come calling with very short notice – and secondly, to check that the arms and armour were serviceable and not being borrowed from another man. A view of individual companies by their own captain often took place before a general muster so that he could see which of his men were still alive and fit and what state their equipment was in. At this point a muster book or roll would be written up for sending to the muster master or one of the deputy lieutenants for use at the general muster which would follow.

A muster roll first used at Totnes, Devonshire, on 20 October 1614 was reused in 1619 or 1620.[8] It contained the names of 125 people, men and women, who were charged with providing a total of 38 corslets, 91 muskets, 54 calivers and 28 halberds. The list was annotated with certain details at this later muster, and included those who were absent due to being at sea (two men), out of town (three men), or dead (12 men). All three categories were

---

4   Surrey History Centre, 6729/13/106.
5   British Library Harley MS 703, f.142.
6   Mary Anne Everett Green (ed.), *Calendar of State Papers, Domestic Series, of the Reign of James I. 1611–1618* (London: 1858; Liechtenstein: Kraus Reprint Ltd, 1967), p.258.
7   British Library Harley MS 703, f.158.
8   Devon Heritage Centre, 3799M/3/O/4-42.

noted as being defaulters. The muster was a view of the arms and armour with no evidence of training taking place.

The Constable of Addingham in the West Riding of Yorkshire paid out 8s 6d for the village's six trained soldiers, who attended a muster held on 23 and 24 April 1626.[9] He also paid out 22d for a pound of powder that was required. Of note is the payment he also made on 24 April, of 8d to borrow some armour. Additional costs were 8d for having the village's armour carried to the muster and home again, 5d for having a sword dressed and 5s 6d for two bandoleers. The purchase of powder indicates that training and exercising took place.

General Musters, Training and Exercising

Not all the training took place at the general musters. The Lord Lieutenant of Shropshire wrote to his deputies on 26 September 1618 to tell them that he had ordered a building to be erected within the castle at Ludlow, to be used as a riding academy;[10] he had also selected a man from Warwickshire whom he considered to be one of the best riders in the country to give instruction in horseriding to young gentlemen. The Warwickshire man had agreed to house six to eight great horses of his own there and Lord Compton had agreed to place 12 or more of his own there as well. He wanted his deputies to pay 40s a year for his keep, and in return their sons would receive training. He also intended to charge all those charged with providing a horse to the trained band to pay 10s a year, for which their horse and rider would be trained with no further payment.

Prior to a general muster, in most if not all the counties, the lord lieutenant or the deputy lieutenants would write up a set of instructions to be followed at the musters. These could include instructions on behaviour or dictate what training was to be carried out and by whom. These instructions varied year on year and were evidently based on what had happened in previous years. They would also contain any new rules from the Privy Council. It would seem that not many of these instructions have survived; so far the present author has found six sets of instructions for musters, one from Wiltshire, four from Devon and one from Essex.

The first set come from Devon and dates to 8 August 1599, a few years before the period under study but still relevant.[11] These instructions were drawn up by the regimental colonels and relate to the behaviour of both the officers and the soldiers. They do not contain any details on what training was required:

Articles set down by the Colonels to be observed upon such penalties as here under are set down:

---

9   West Yorkshire Archives Service, 49D90/3/1.
10   Historical Manuscripts Commission, *Tenth Report*, p.366.
11   Devon Heritage Centre, 3799M-3/O/2/23.

That all Captains & all other inferior officers shall observe and obey all commands from the Colonels.

That no inferior officer shall misdemean himself against any of his superior officers upon pain of imprisonment or otherwise at the Colonel's pleasure to lose his place.

That no officer shall be drunk or known to keep whores upon pain of imprisonment & also to be cashiered from his place & disarmed out of this town of garrison.

That no soldier shall run away from his colours upon pain of death.

That no soldier absent himself from the watch or ward upon pain of imprisonment.

That no soldier abuse himself in his watch or ward upon pain of imprisonment.

That no soldier make any noise as shooting of pieces or sounding of drums or any such like or keep any ill order in the street, tavern or alehouse, in the evening after the watch is set till the next morning it shall be discharged upon pain of imprisonment & loss of ten days pay.

That no soldier sell or try to pawn any of his arms, furniture or munition there unto appertaining upon pain of one month's imprisonment & the loss of forty days pay.

That no soldier depart of this town above & also a mile without the special license of their Colonel, Captain or some of their inferior officers, upon pain of imprisonment.

That no soldier shall resist or strike any officer within this town of garrison or in his march upon pain of losing his hand.

That no soldier shall be usually drunk upon pain of one month's imprisonment.

That no soldier shall swear upon pain of loss of so much pay as the Colonel shall think convenient.

The next set of instructions come from Wiltshire and are dated to October 1617.[12] These were drawn up by the deputy lieutenants for use at the next muster, subject to the approval of the lord lieutenant. They cover the qualifications of those who were charged with providing the arms and armour, attendance and use of munitions:

---

12   Hampshire Record Office, 44M69/G5/36/3.

Certain points agreed upon at Marlborough primo October 1617 concerning musters & furnitures of the trained bands. If the Right Honourable, the Lord Lieutenant of this county shall be pleased to allow thereof.

Perfect rolls to be made & delivered to the colonels & captains agreeing with our book and so reserve to ourselves counter part of those rolls thereby to call the musters.

The musters of the soldiers henceforth to be taken under the colonels' and captains' colours and not otherwise.

Sixteen supplies to be brought to every muster of every hundred's soldiers to be paid so by the said captains & allowed us.

That no soldier shall be admitted to serve the Trained Bands but such as shall have £2 per annum in lands [secured] for term of his life or 21 years in [possession] or £10 in [rental] or in goods to the value of £40.

That every soldier which [shows] for himself or any other shall bear his own charges to the musters.

That such as are absent from musters shall be punished according to the Statute. If reasonable excuse be made at the musters.

That the Muster Master's entertainment be paid by those which are charged with the finding of arms &furnitures & the names of such persons which shall refuse to pay shall be certified to the Lord Lieutenant that order may be taken for the reformation thereof by his Lordship's authority.

Touching such as have land in two shires. Our opinions are that they which have land in this county of Wiltshire shall find arms according to the means they have here and not excused themselves by finding arms in any other shire according to their whole estate.

To avoid the waste & spoil of powder & match it is agreed that the soldiers shall receive the powder & match in the field from those that are or shall be appointed to have the same in readiness, viz, 3lbs for every musket & 1lb for every caliver, and [every] soldier shall bring his powder or match with him.

A third set of instructions comes from Devon, and was issued for the musters held in March 1619. A number of points are worth highlighting. It was ordered that defective weapons were not to be broken but sent back to the local constable for replacement. This indicates that breaking was the previous method of dealing with defective weapons. The measures taken to deter the borrowing of arms and armour by keeping the men in place during the muster, and holding the county musters on the same day, were a serious effort. Lastly, the inclusion of men provided by the clergy in the local companies shows a determination to bring the clergy into line with the rest of the county.

Instructions for George Gale, gentleman, Muster Master General of the forces in the county of Devon by such to be observed and duly performed in and through all the Regiments and particular companies of the same according to certain orders agreed upon by me, William, Earl of Bath, his Majesty's Lieutenant General of the said county and my Deputy Lieutenants at Okehampton, the 26th of February last for the taking of a general view and muster of all the forces within my Lieutenancy as follows;

Imprimis, whereas the said view and muster is for diverse good and valuable reasons appointed to be taken all in one day vizt, on Tuesday the 23rd of this instant March at the several places specified in the foot of these instructions, you therefore, the said Muster Master shall by writing under your hand and seal institute so many able and sufficient persons to be your deputies or commissaries during this service as that there may be one in every place of muster where yourself cannot be present to see that these articles following be put in execution and duly performed the which I require both you and them in his Majesty's name carefully to observe as you will answer the contrary at your perils.

1. That every several company be placed in Battalion, a good distance one from the other and then you [are] to take the names of the officers thereof together with the number of pikes and shot.

2. [two words faded] the files and ranks stand in their open order you pass through them recording what arms or part of arms or other defective or wanting together with the names of the owners thereof.

3. That so soon as you have mustered any company, you cause the clerk of the band to call the said company by his muster book and to give you the names of those that are absent and their places of abode, the which you are to constitute unto to me.

4. That for preventing of borrowing of arms you take special care that no man depart out of his rank with his arms until all the companies be mustered.

5. That to this end, the muster be not in any town but in the fields and that whilst one company is mustering the rest exercised by their captains and officers.

6. That the forces of the clergy be reduced into the Bands of their several captains that have command of the laity in the said parishes and that their defects be certified unto me with the rest in manner aforesaid.

7. That in case there be any arms altogether defective in part or in whole you do not break the said arms but deliver them to the constable of the parish where the owner thereof dwells with charge that he do not deliver therein until the owner

has bought other sufficient arms and that you certify the constables name to whom you have delivered them.

8. That you allow not of any calivers or unfit arms, but certify therein [if any such be] as defects.

9. That you command of the constables of hundreds a perfect roll or book, fair written, of the names of all the able untrained men within their divisions from the age of 18 to 60 and bring the same to the Muster Master together with your certificate.

10. That you give warning to the said constables to collect the Muster Master's fee now due for one half year after the rate of a hundred marks per annum according to the last order and to bring the same at his lodging at one Brimblecombe's house within Northgate in Exeter on Thursday the eight of April next coming by eight of the clock in the forenoon.

11. That you, the deputies or commissaries, do send your several certificates of all the particulars above required to the Muster Master at his said lodging in Exeter on Friday the 26th of this instant March and you the said Muster Master to return unto me at my house at Tavistock your roll and general certificate of all yours and your commissaries proceedings by the said month.

The next set of instructions also came from Devon and these were for the musters in 1620.[13] As stated earlier, the instructions were based on the requirements for the current year combined with anything carried over from the previous year. This year's instructions focused on the men in the trained bands and the reserves in the county. Of note is the reference to the musketeers being trained, once a month, to shoot at a mark. This is possibly as a result of poor shooting the year before. The appointment of a treasurer is of interest, quite large sums of money needing to be raised to finance these musters. The theft of the powder is unusual, and is the only reference the present author has seen to such an action. The text of the instructions is as follows:

Item, that the constables of Hundreds at the same day so bring to the Muster Master's Commissary a perfect roll of the names of all the untrained bands within their several divisions from the age of 18 years to 60, of able men, and being fairly written in a book to be delivered to the Muster Master and by him to the Lord Lieutenant, whereof notice is forthwith to be given by every several colonel throughout their regiment that the constables may have sufficient time to make up their books accordingly.

Item, that in the choice of trained men those of the better sort and quality be not exempted, but enrolled in the several bands with their arms. And that the forces of the clergy be likewise mustered therewith.

---

13 Devon Heritage Centre, 3799M-3/O/2/41.

Item, that the beacons and beacon houses be forthwith fully repaired.

That the colonels of every regiment do presently appoint captains and officers for the untrained bands allotting 200 men to each captain who are thereupon as speedily as may be to see the soldiers sufficiently armed and a roll thereof made. That the musketeers be monthly exercised to shoot with bullet at a mark during this summer, on days and at places most convenient for the most ease of the county.

That two or three fit men be appointed in every parish by the constables of the said parishes to be foot posts for conveyance of letters upon all occasions.

Sir William Strode to be treasurer for the War throughout the county and it is ordered that the head constables shall at Michaelmas sessions next, bring unto him their several accounts of all the money which they have or shall receive, or disburse for the martial service for the year past.

That the towns assigned to have proportions of powder in store do sell the same to the country at 12d the pound or under when there shall be need. And the Deputy Lieutenants next residing to any of the towns that are to have store of powder do see from time to time that the proportions agreed on the 26th of February 1618, be always in readiness in the said towns.

That every person set to a musket be always provided of 3 pound of powder, 3 pound of bullets and 2 pound of match for each musket, and the charge thereof to be raised upon the whole parish.

Item, whereas there was a quantity of powder lately stolen out of the storehouse at Culliton [5 miles SW of Axminster]. It is ordered that the same shall be supplied at the general charge of the 5 hundreds of St Mary Ottery, Cliston, East Dudleigh, Axminster and Culliton.

Item, that the charge of the soldiers' pay after 8d per diem, the pay of the officers, the charge of the powder used, at the general muster be cast into one total sum and proportionately levied within every division as the Muster Master's fee is usually paid.

Item, that the colonels do give order to their several captains to view their companies at such time and places as shall be most convenient for the ease of the country to the end that all defects may be supplied against the general muster.

The final set of instructions from Devon were for the county musters held in 1621:

Orders and instructions set down the 12th of April 1621 for a general muster within the county commanded by letters from the Lords of his Majesty's most honourable Privy Council dated the last of February 1620.

That every several regiment shall be mustered and trained by the colonels or their deputies and officers and the Muster Master or his commissary on Tuesday and Wednesday the 22nd and 23rd of May next at the places following, vizt;

Item, that in the choice of trained men those of the better sort and quality be not exempted, but enrolled and serve with the rest.

That Sir William Strode be Treasurer General throughout the county and that the Head Constables do at Michaelmas sessions next, bring unto him their several accounts of all the money which they have received or disbursed for the martial service for the year present and that such as failed to bring in their account last year, do then bring them and present their accounts as the rest do.

That every person set to a musket be always provided of 3 pound of powder, 3 pound of bullets and 2 pound of match for each musket, and the charge thereof to be raised upon the whole parish.

That the charge of the soldiers' pay after 8d per diem, the officers' pay and the charge of powder used, at the general muster be cast into one total sum and levied proportionately within every division as the Muster Master's fee is levied.

That the colonels give order to their several captains to view their companies and see that all things be supplied that are defective against the said muster.

That the towns assigned to have proportions of powder in store do sell the same to the country at 12d the pound or under when there shall be need.

The towns that are to have the said powder in store & the Deputies that are appointed to view the same.

To be viewed by Sir William Courteney or such as he shall appoint twice every year or so often as he shall think fit.

The last set of muster instructions come from Essex for the year 1626.[14] These were intended for the soldiers and the finders of arms, and were issued to the Essex constables on 1 August 1626 by the Lord Lieutenant and his deputies, as follows.

That no person standing charged with finding arms was to fail in sending those arms and the soldiers to the usual places for training with powder and match. And that no soldier was to leave his colours until he was discharged by his captain and that no man was to borrow any arms or armour but was at all times to have his arms and armour with him ready at an hour's notice upon pain of severe punishment if he was discovered.

No soldier should leave his place of abode without first obtaining a licence from the deputy lieutenant of his division.

---

14 Essex Record Office, D/B 3/3/201.

Every musketeer should have his bandoleer full of powder which should be renewed every day. He should also have 24 bullets and six yards of match and a knapsack to carry the bullets and match in as well as his victuals. All was to be paid for by the people charged with providing the arms and armour. Each musketeer was also to have a bullet mould which matched the bore of his musket.

Lastly, every soldier should always be at an hour's notice ready to move, with his arms and provisions, to his colours at the rendezvous as chosen by his captain.

Length of Service

The solders did not serve for a set period of time in the trained bands. At every muster the soldiers who had served the previous year were expected to be present unless there was a good reason for their absence. Valid reasons for being absent included death, disability and leaving the county with the permission of at least one deputy lieutenant. Looking at the muster certificates for a number of counties gives some idea of the length of time soldiers served. Table 18 shows the Northamptonshire, returns for five of the county's hundreds for the years 1632 and 1634 to 1636.[15]

Table 18. Northamptonshire hundreds' muster returns 1632, 1634–1636

	Nr of years attending musters	Nr soldiers attending musters	% of soldiers attending musters
One year	1	37	18.5%
Two years	2	26	13.0%
Three years	3	27	13.5%
Four years	4	110	55.0%
Total		200	100%

Although we do not have the figures for 1633, it can be assumed that those who attended four annual musters almost certainly attended in 1633 and a proportion of those who attended in 1632 and 1634 would also have been present in 1633. This shows that over half of the soldiers received training for at least five years and probably more.

James and Charles were very keen that the training in the counties should be standardised, and to this end they periodically sent out training manuals to the lord lieutenants to pass on to the deputies and then the trained band officers. This practice was intended to make sure that the latest methods were being taught to the officers and soldiers. Two examples of contemporary training manuals are shown in Appendices V and VI. In 1628 Charles went a step further and announced that the horse were to be gathered into four

---

15   Northamptonshire Record Office, CA7506, Cartwright Muster Book.

musters which he would attend personally, so that he could see them being trained. The quality and the quantity of the horse was an ongoing problem throughout this period.

Actual training of the men, foot and horse, was supposed to be carried out at a number of levels, and this was reiterated by the Privy Council on a number of occasions. At the bottom were the captains of the companies, these men, when issued with their commissions were made aware that they would be personally responsible for the training of their men.

Sometimes the captain would train part of his company, usually when these men were in a town or borough with a charter. For that reason they often insisted on being trained in the town or borough. For the Leicestershire county muster in 1615, the Lord Lieutenant informed the Mayor of Leicester that the men selected to serve as the town's soldiers had to be mustered on 12 October, "by 9 o'clock". Leicester's Corporation paid 3d for three "queyre" of brown paper to weigh up the gunpowder for the training.

Before the muster, the captain would send out a warning letter or warrant to those towns where he was to train their soldiers. These were usually the towns that would not send their soldiers to musters with the other soldiers, which meant the rest of the company coming to them. An example of one of these letters is shown in Appendix IV; this is from Essex for the town of Maldon.

The training did not always go according to plan. An incident occurred in Norfolk on 29 March 1619, at a company muster held at Belaugh, north-east of Norwich.[16] The report on the incident was written up on 25 April by Henry Seaman, possibly one of the company's officers. In the report, Seaman writes that Henry Deroniye is charged with bringing a musket charged with a bullet onto the muster field, and confirms that this had been done at Seaman's own request so that he could check the piece by having it fired. The firer was not near the rest of the company and Henry Seaman was willing to testify to this if it was needed.

Many of the captains held their post not due to military experience but because of their social status. A set of instructions for them could often have been used. A handwritten set of instructions from Hampshire dated to about 1627 and entitled *The Exercising of a Foot Company* gives guidance on training musketeers to fire.[17] The writer says:

> For the shooting at a mark there must be a halberd set up where the soldiers must begin their postures and another halberd some twenty paces off, and the mark some two hundred and twenty or 200 and 50 paces off. Every soldier when he hath shot must fall in the rear of his own file.

> There must be always commandment given to the musketeers that they have always small dry priming powder.

---

16   The National Archives, SP 14/108, f.113.
17   Hampshire Record Office, 44M69/G5/48/1, f.5.

To command them also that they lock their matches long enough for else the weight of the match behind holds that the lock will not come home in the pan.

A measure charge must be given to every soldier that holds just as much powder as half the bullet weight at ten to the pound to fit his charge of the bandoleer.

Sometimes the lord lieutenant of a county would be keen that his subordinates do a good job. In a letter sent from Edward Conway, Lord Lieutenant of Hampshire, to his deputy lieutenants on 24 November 1625, Conway spoke of Charles' great desire to establish an "Exact Militia",[18] and wanted Hampshire to take the lead in perfecting its trained band, emphasising that the county was a prime target for an invader; he offered to arrange a supply of arms and armour to replace any items that were defective, naturally at a reasonable rate. He also offered to send experienced soldiers to train the captains and other officers.

Lord Conway wrote to his deputies again on 6 January 1626. With the letter he sent a number of copies of a book for exercising the soldiers, and "a rule whereby to govern yourselves for making good the propositions of arms which by sale, leases, division of lands, dowries or the like have been diminished and in some parts altogether lost". He also arranged to send an understanding soldier to train the captains and other officers. Of note was the offer that Lord Conway made to pay for this man himself, who was in addition to the expected arrival of the Low Country soldiers being sent to train the trained bands. In his letter Conway also promised to have those men from the county who were "certified to be refractory" to be sent for and be put in prison pending their appearance before the Council.

In 1631 Nathaniel Stevens in Gloucestershire was issued his commission from one of the deputy lieutenants.[19] The part relating to training reads as follows:

These are therefore by virtue of the said commission to authorise you, Nathaniel Stevens, esquire, from time to time, as often as you shall see sufficient cause, at least twice yearly to assemble, muster and call together to such place or places, as you shall think convenient, all that company of foot heretofore under your conduct and command.

A captain could call upon the county muster master for assistance in training his men, and even one or more of the deputy lieutenants.

On 31 May 1631 the Privy Council wrote to the Lord Lieutenant of Cambridge regarding the annual musters.[20] In the letter they explained that musters should be held at least once a year, as per their instructions sent out in 1629 and again in 1630. Some unnamed counties, however, had not sent in a return for two or three years and so the Privy Council felt obliged to send out the order for a muster every year. They required the lord lieutenants'

---

18   Hampshire Record Office, 44M69/G5/37/1/1 & 4.
19   Gloucestershire Archives, D547a/F6.
20   British Library Harley MS 4014, ff.12, 13.

return by 1 October. The Lord Lieutenant duly wrote to his deputies on 4 July to inform them that a muster was required by the Privy Council and enclosed a copy of their letter.

On 30 April 1632 the Privy Council wrote to the Lord Lieutenant of Cambridge repeating their complaint that some counties had not sent in their returns for two or three years, though again not naming them. However they reiterated that Cambridge was to hold a muster and send in a return by 30 October.[21] They also noted that although they only expected annual musters they did expect the captains to exercise their men on holidays or at other times when they might "spend their time drinking & unlawful exercise", and also on some days to train their whole company together with the agreement of the deputy lieutenants. The Privy Council also noted that the only men exempt from service in the trained band were the King's menial servants or those who "have such place under the King as may lawfully excuse him". After the annual muster in 1632 the Lord Lieutenant complained to the Privy Council about a number of men who were refusing to attend the muster, and about others who were refusing to provide arms.[22]

The musters were held at places which were as convenient as possible for all concerned. Where a company or regiment was raised in a single hundred then a location within that hundred was used. A good example of this is the county of Lancashire. Each hundred provided a company of 100 men, their muster points were as shown on Map 2.

Attendance

An ongoing problem with the musters was attendance. Sending orders or writing letters to men requiring their attendance did not always work, nor did threats. A letter sent to the Lord Lieutenant of Leicestershire in October 1637 illustrates this problem very well.[23] This referred to the muster of Captain Rooe's Company of approximately 200 men. The writer, probably one of the deputy lieutenants, complained that one of the towns, Enderby, refused to provide the arms for one of its soldiers. Regarding the private soldiers in the company, eight were absent while three other men refused to hire a man to serve and simply sent their servants to the musters. The clergy were also mentioned, with three of them being named for never sending to the musters the two corselets that they were charged with. This was not uncommon for the musters in every county.

The situation with the horse was even worse. In Gloucester in 1625, of the 20 light horse which should have been at the muster only 10 were there,[24] and of those 10, one was deemed to be insufficient. In the same year in Sussex the deputy lieutenants wrote to the lord lieutenants to inform them that the horse were in a bad way, were few in number, the arms and armour were poor and

---

21 British Library, Harley MS 4014, ff. 14, 15.
22 1632, Calendar of State Papers, Domestic Series, Vol. CCXXX, p.500.
23 Leicestershire Record Office, 1669–1885.
24 Gloucestershire Archives GBR/H2/2, pp. 59–60.

Map 2. County map of Lancashire showing the muster points used by the foot companies. (Mapping software kindly provided by the Cambridge Group, the ESRC, the Leverhulme Trust and the British Academy and produced by Derek Tate)

the horses not up to the task required. The deputies wanted the lord lieutenants to personally intervene with the defaulters, to force them to do their duty.[25]

Precedence

When more than one company was present at a muster there had to be a precedence for marching into the field; so far the present author has found two examples of this, one from Lancashire and the other from the Isle of Wight. Regarding Lancashire, the lord lieutenant required the precedence to be based upon the hundred that the trained band companies came from, which was to be as follows: Derby, Amoundernes, Blackburn, Leyland, Salford and Lonsdale, this probably dates to 1626. They were to go into the field and to come out, the first in pike order,[26] though was not explained further. There was no order of precedence for the untrained companies. Regarding the Isle of Wight, in March 1629 the Lord Lieutenant wrote to the two deputy lieutenants advising them of the seniority or precedence of the captains in the two regiments or divisions on the island.[27] The Lord Lieutenant insisted that the seniority of the captains in his list be followed.

Drummers

In 1635 the Privy Council gave instructions to the Lord Lieutenant of Cambridgeshire that a new march was to be used by the drummers.[28] This was the "English March" and was to be used in this country and by those men serving abroad in the pay of other countries. This order was to be passed to the deputy lieutenants and by them to the captains of all the companies. On 1 June 1636 the King issued a warrant to John Rudd appointing him to instruct all the drummers, or drum beaters, in the trained bands in all the counties of England and Wales.[29] A transcript of the warrant is at Appendix III. He, or one of his deputies, was to instruct the drummers on the "English March", he was also to ascertain how many drummers each trained band company needed. The Lord Lieutenant of Cambridgeshire was to arrange a suitable fee for John Rudd or for whichever of his deputies was instructing their drummers. On the 14 June the Lord Lieutenant sent a copy of John Rudd's warrant to the deputy lieutenants. They were to assist him or his deputies in their task of instructing the county's drummers in the use of the "English March" and they were to ensure that he, or his deputies, were suitably recompensed. A Mr Rudd, Drum Major, was buried in York on 2 July 1644, possibly the same man.

---

25 Sussex Archaeological Society, Lewes, 1896, Volume 40, page 13.
26 Lancashire Record Office, DDN-1-64, Deputy Lieutenant's Book.
27 Sir Richard Worsley, *The History of the Isle of Wight* (London: 1781; reprint 1975, E.P. Publishing Ltd), appendix xv.
28 British Library Harley MS 4014, f.19.
29 British Library Harley MS 4014, ff. 22, 23

Shooting Practise

Every town and village in England and Wales was supposed to have a set of butts erected so that, originally, the men could practise archery. With the advent of firearms the requirement for a set of butts continued. There are many references to money being paid out for the erection, repair or maintenance of the butts in town and village constables' accounts. So far the present author has seen only one description of a set of butts, this document is dated to 1585, but it was intended to be used for firearms training so it is unlikely the design would have changed very much as calivers were replaced with muskets. The document comes from Northamptonshire, and was sent to Sir Christopher Hatton along with his commission as Lord Lieutenant of Northamptonshire in 1586.[30] It is entitled *Directions for the Corporals* and reads as follows (the spelling has been updated):

> That for every corporal there may be a butt of 20 feet broad and 16 feet high erected in some convenient place remote from the highway or other common frequented place and in the midst thereof to set a roundel of board of a yard and a half broad with certain black roundels and a white in the midst against which the soldier is to level his piece for his better aim and ready discharging.

> That the soldier be placed 150 paces from the said butt and instructed how to stand comely in his piece, and that he find his mark readily through the sight of his piece and to know how to bring the pin standing upon the mouth of his piece, his mark and sight of his piece, all into one direct line.

> That every soldier shall be limited by the said corporal how many shot he shall discharge, above which number he may not shoot.

Included in the instructions for the musters in Devon for 1620 were the requirements for the musketeers' training.[31] The musketeers were to be "monthly exercised to shoot with bullet at a mark during this summer, on days and at places most convenient for the most ease of the county".

On 20 November 1624 the lord lieutenants of Derbyshire informed the Privy Council that they had mustered and trained their soldiers. This training had included weapon handling, drill and for the musketeers, shooting at marks.[32]

Part of the Warwick Trained Band was mustered at Meriden, located between Coventry and Birmingham, on 24 July 1626. The musketeers were issued with barrel number 6, containing 107 lb of old gunpowder from the

---

30 Jeremy Goring and Joan Wake (eds), *Northamptonshire Lieutenancy Papers and Other Documents 1580–1614*, (Gateshead: Northamptonshire Record Society, 1975), p.18; also, Joan Wake (ed.), *A Copy of Papers Relating to Musters, Beacons, Subsidies etc., in the County of Northampton, AD 1586–1623*, vol. III (Kettering: Northamptonshire Record Society, 1926), p.7.

31 Devon Heritage Centre, 3799M-3/O/2/41.

32 20 Nov 1624, Latimers, CSPD, Vol. CLXXV, p.384.

Coventry storehouse to use in the training.[33] Further training was carried out at Warwick on 27 July, with barrel number 28 being used, also containing 107 lb of old gunpowder from the Coventry storehouse. At Wolston on 3 August barrel number 3 was used with 107 lb of powder, and lastly barrel number 32 with 110 lb of powder was used at the muster at Stratford on the Thursday following, 4 August.

In an order sent out in 1635 by the Council of War there is a brief mention of training the cavalry's horses for battle.[34] The groom should dress the horse, give him his fodder on the drum head and while the horse is eating discharge a pistol. It was also recommended that the horse be trained to charge a set of armour set on a stake, knock it over and trample it. They were also instructed to ensure that the cavalry were trained at least once per month, but there is little or no evidence that this took place.

The Soldiers' Pay

Leicester was paying its soldiers 8 pence (d) per day of training from at least 1606. However, they were also paid 4d each for "prize money" and another 1d each over and above their pay.[35] For the muster held in the town from 12 to 14 October 1615 Leicester fielded 40 soldiers; each of these men was paid 1s per day they trained.[36] From 1619 the town actually paid the men 16d per day while training, 4d more than anywhere else.

For the Northamptonshire musters in 1613 held at Kettering, the deputy lieutenants ordered that the towns and men charged with providing arms and money were to pay five shillings (s) per trained soldier. The accounts for the two days of training tell us that the soldiers themselves were paid 1s per day while the sergeants, corporals and musicians were paid 5s per day. The captain was paid for an extra day and received £5 in total, the lieutenant £1 per day and the ensign or ancient, 10s per day.[37]

In August 1633 four of the Suffolk deputy lieutenants agreed rates of pay for the county's trained bands, both horse and foot.[38] These were as shown in Tables 19 and 20.

At the muster held in Middlesex on 18 June 1635, the captains decided to raise a number of issues with the deputy lieutenants.[39] The captains of the foot companies were complaining about the amount of money they had to pay their officers, sergeants, corporals and drummers at the musters. This was paid at every muster, Shrove Tuesdays, May Days and other days by special order. The daily pay for their men was 20s to the lieutenants, 15s to the ensigns, 10s for the sergeants and corporals and 5s for the drummers.

33 Coventry History Centre, BA/H/17/A79/146a, dated 4 August 1626.
34 Rye, State papers relating to musters, p.203.
35 Leicestershire Record Office, Records of the Borough of Leicester, BR/III/2/75, f.31.
36 Leicestershire Record Office, Records of the Borough of Leicester, BR/II/18/12, f.2.
37 Publications of the Northamptonshire Record Society, Vol. VII, Peterborough, 1935, p.87.
38 Bodleian Library MS Tanner 71, f.168.
39 The National Archives, SP 16/312, f.128.

Table 19. The pay for the officers of the horse

For the Lieutenant	12s a day
For the Cornet	10s a day
For the Clerk of the Band	6s 4d a day
For the two Trumpeters	5s a piece a day
For the 3 Corporals	5s a piece each day
Sum total for the officers of the horse amounts to	53s 4d

Table 20. The pay for the officers of the foot

For the Lieutenant	10s a day
For the Ancient	6s 8d a day
For 4 sergeants	3s 4d a day
For 3 Corporals	1s 6d a day
For 3 Drums	2s 6d a day
For the Clerk of the Band	8s a day
Sum total for the officers of the foot amounts;	£2 10s

The soldiers were also complaining about the cost of their apparel and arms: they were obliged to pay for their powder and match at every muster and every time they were put into the field for other reasons, and the cost of powder had increased from 12d a pound to 20d a pound. The officers, notwithstanding the captains' complaints, said that their pay was insufficient considering the number of times they were called out. Finally, a complaint was made that there were many men who could pay towards the cost of the horse but did not, and their age exempted them from serving in the foot companies. It was suggested that there could be an order from the Privy Council allowing them to be charged or levied as this was for the defence of the realm. The muster certificate was sent in on 29 January 1636 to the Lord Lieutenants and included all the complaints made to the deputies.

On 26 September 1626 the City of Worcester decided to start paying its trained soldiers 12d a day.[40] Prior to this the men had not been paid. It was noted, however, that they were still liable for paying their share of the assessment for their pay thus they were effectively paying in part of their pay and then receiving it back.

---

40   Bond, *The Chamber Order Book of Worcester, 1602–50*, p.207.

The County Muster Masters

In Barriffe's *Military Discipline or the Young Artilleryman*, there is a poem of sorts which relates to the county muster masters and the trained band captains quite well:

> You that have eyes to read, and skill to judge
> And have perus'd these doublings I have done
> Though I have tedious been, yet do not grudge
> For you know well, I have skipt over some
> But marvel not; the cause I do not show them
> It is not much material for to know them
>
> Those that are skilful in the Art of Warre
> And take delight to exercise their men
> Shall find more pleasure in these doublings farre
> If that they intermix them now and then
> And so contrive their doublings in these cases
> That lastly one word brings them to their places
>
> Why in our country do we captains chuse
> That have no skill nor artful inclination
> They do themselves and country much abuse
> Thus to deceive them in their expectation
> I think the cause of this fault in our nation
> Is, that our country holds it not in fashion
>
> But some, perhaps, will say, I am too bold
> There's no such need for captains to have skill
> The Muster Masters have enough (some hold)
> The captains and the counties for to fill
> So whilst the Muster Master doth the labour
> The officers may play upon a tabour
>
> But stay! Me thinks, one pulls me by the sleeve
> And tells me that I have myself forgot
> Whereof doublings, here I take my leave
> Entreating those that read, mistake me not
> Let Muster Masters take their money, then
> But let the captains exercise their men

Each county was supposed to have its own muster master, and one problem which seemed to affect many counties was the reluctance of the residents to pay for his services. On 21 December 1619 the Privy Council wrote to the Earl of Northampton, Lord Lieutenant of Warwickshire and Lord President of Wales, to tell him to make sure that anyone refusing to pay their assessment towards the muster master's pay in those areas under his jurisdiction were to be reported to the Privy Council.[41] On 21 December 1629 the Privy Council sent out a letter to the lord lieutenants regarding the standard of the county trained bands and their thoughts as to why they were not as good as they should be. They said that one problem was that the muster masters were not training the soldiers in some counties, because they were not being paid. The Privy Council included a "job description" for the role of muster master to the lord lieutenants of all the counties. The main requirements of the post were as follows.

Firstly, he was to ensure that the men serving in the trained bands were physically able, if they were not he was to liaise with one or more of the deputy lieutenants to get replacements.

Secondly, he was to ensure that the weapons and other equipment shown at the musters was serviceable and was the soldiers' own and not borrowed from other soldiers.

Thirdly, he was to be available to help the captains train their men in their duties and postures not just at the musters but also at other convenient times.

Finally he was to reside in the county where he was the muster master and be available for duty when summoned by the lord lieutenant or one or more of the deputy lieutenants for training or other duties. He was to be an experienced soldier of good reputation and able to perform his duties, if he was not then he should be dismissed.[42]

These men were paid differing amounts, with the money being raised by a levy on the whole county on those providing the arms and armour or by charging the trained band soldiers a fixed sum at the musters.

There were many issues in most if not all the counties, and some of these have been included here to illustrate.

The Muster Master, Cambridge

On 2 January 1630 the Lord Lieutenant of Cambridgeshire wrote to his deputies regarding a letter from the Privy Council dated 21 December 1629.[43] The letter concerned the training of the trained band and especially the muster master. The Privy Council understood that in a number of counties the trained bands, horse and foot, were defective due to a lack of training, which they attributed to the muster masters not doing their job, or in some cases not doing their job because they were not getting paid. The Lord Lieutenant or his deputies were to ensure that the muster master did his duty diligently, and the Privy Council sent a list of tasks that were to be completed by him:

Firstly, he was to ensure that the soldiers in the Trained Band were fit and the right sort of men, if not he was to inform the deputies so that unfit men could be replaced.

---

41 J.V. Lyle (ed.), *Acts of the Privy Council of England*, Volume 37, 1619–1621 (London: HMSO, 1930), pp.94–5.

42 Dasent, *Acts of the Privy Council of England, 1629, May–1630 May*, pp.213–4, and The National Archives, PC 2/39, f.553.

43 British Library Harley MS 4014, ff. 8, 9.

Secondly, he was to check that the men's arms and armour were serviceable and not borrowed from someone else.

Thirdly, he was to assist the captains in training their men to use their arms and their postures, not just at the general musters but also at other, convenient, times.

Fourthly, he was to reside in the county that he served, that he should be an experienced soldier with combat experience on the Continent and have testimonies to prove this.

Finally, since so much was expected of the muster master, if the current man holding that post was deemed unable to do these tasks then he should be replaced by a man who was. The Lord Lieutenant or the deputies were to meet and send in a certificate detailing how much the previous muster master had been paid and how the money had been collected for payment. This was to be done by 20 February.

The Lord Lieutenant informed the deputies that their return should be with him or the Privy Council by 20 February.

The Muster Master, Durham

On 28 October 1618 a levy of 2d in the pound was ordered to be collected to pay Captain Hodson for the current year and for his arrears of pay.[44] The four probable deputy lieutenants wrote to the Bishop on 20 April 1619 to give their support for the continuance of Captain Hodson as the county's Muster Master:[45] in their opinion he had been of service to the county in the mustering and training of the trained band which he had been doing for eight years. This letter was probably used by him to support his petition to the Privy Council to obtain his arrears of pay from the Bishop.[46] In his petition he noted that the King had recommended him to the post nine years previously and he had been accepted. Now, however, the legality of his position was being challenged by Sir Henry Anderson, MP, an associate of Talbot Bowes, one of the probable deputy lieutenants.[47] Sir Henry was demanding to know by what statute the office of the muster master was established; the local JP, Judge Hutton, had said that it was established by Royal Prerogative and that that was sufficient. Sir Henry, however, was maintaining that the muster master's post and his allowance were illegal and the Bishop was blocking his pay although the warrant for it had been approved by the deputy lieutenants.

The Muster Master, Northumberland

The Privy Council wrote to the Mayor and Aldermen of Newcastle on 24 February 1617 concerning a petition from Captain Thomas Jackson.[48] He was the muster master of the town but despite all his efforts the town had not paid him. The Privy Council informed the Mayor and Aldermen that

44 Green, *Calendar of State Papers, Domestic Series, 1611–1618*, p.587.
45 The National Archives, SP 14/7108, f.95.
46 The National Archives, SP 14/7108, f.93.
47 <https://www.historyofparliamentonline.org/volume/1604-1629/member/anderson-sir-henry-15823-1659>, accessed 08/03/20
48 The National Archives, PC 2/28, f.559.

they were to pay his arrears and were to continue to employ him as it was important for a port town such as theirs to have a trained and disciplined force available. By 1619 Captain Jackson was describing himself as the muster master for Northumberland and he was still not being paid, his current rate of pay was now £40 per year.[49] In 1619 he petitioned the Treasury for a warrant to have his arrears paid by the Treasury Receiver General in Yorkshire; it seems that the newly appointed Treasurer was not aware that Jackson had been receiving warrants for his pay from the two previous Treasurers. The wording of the petition indicates that he was employed by the Privy Council as muster master and not by the county. The wording was as follows, "the petitioner's former honest services and his employment by the honourable Lords of the Council as Muster Master in Northumberland".

The Muster Master Suffolk

In 1613 the deputies were informed that Huntington Colby had been appointed as the county's muster master.[50] In the same year an instruction was issued concerning the muster master's pay: he was to be paid £100 at the musters, this was to be £10 from every foot band when he trained them. Additionally he was to receive £50 every year for viewing the horse companies, and this amount to be paid was broken down as follows: Bury St Edmunds £13 13s 4d, the Liberty of St Andrews, Ipswich, £8 6s 8d and the "Guildables", £25. Ipswich was also to pay an extra £10 for the horse and foot musters. This requirement was sent to the chief constables of the Suffolk hundreds, that for Stow Hundred was sent on 20 May. In this the chief constables were told that their share of "Guildables" amounted to £4 14s 6d, which they were to collect and hand to Sir Lionel Tollemach, captain of the horse troop. They were also to collect the £10 due from the local foot company commanded by Sir Calthrop Parker, this was to be paid to Sir Calthrop at Ipswich on 7 June, the day of this company's muster. Huntington Colby was in the Low Countries by August 1614; the Lord Lieutenant informed his deputies that Philip Colby, his brother, had been appointed in his place while Huntington Colby was absent and was to be paid at the same rate as his brother.

Captain Philip Colby, Esq., served as the county's muster master until at least June 1615.[51] In early July 1616 the Lord Lieutenant informed his deputies that due to Philip Colby being now otherwise employed and his brother Huntington still serving in the Low Countries, he had appointed another of their brothers as the muster master; this brother was Francis Colby.[52] He was to receive the same allowance as his brothers had previously.

On 8 July 1618 the Lord Lieutenant wrote to the deputies to inform them that he had appointed Captain Henry Woodhouse as the county's muster master.[53] He was a veteran of the Isle of Rhé expedition and La Rochelle, and

---

49 The National Archives, SP 14/111, f. 216.
50 British Library Add MS 39245, ff.8, 11–12.
51 Suffolk Record Office, FC85//I1/21.
52 British Library Add MS 39245, f.34.
53 British Library Wodehouse papers. Vol. XXVIII. Letter-books of the Deputy-Lieutenants and Justices of the Peace for co. Suffolk; 1608–1640, ff. 38, 39; British Library, Add MS 39245, f.38.

died in 1637. In 1619 the deputies of Bury St Edmunds wrote to the deputies of the "Guildables" to inform them that they had been visited by Captain Woodhouse.[54] He had told them that in other counties, such as Norfolk, the muster master took command of the musters and viewing and was paid for this. They had refused his services and payment to him as there was no letter from the Lord Lieutenant giving him this authority which they needed to levy money to pay him. They now had such a letter, dated 18 March, and the muster master was to be at their muster at Easter, where he would be in charge and be paid. Captain Woodhouse was not always present in the county, he was absent for the musters held in 1623,[55] and in his absence his deputy, Mr Wentworth, had been appointed to act as muster master. Despite the absence of Captain Woodhouse, the Lord Lieutenant still wanted his arrears of pay to be made good.

By 1624 the issue of the muster master's pay had become a problem in the county.[56] As part of the preparations for the annual general muster some of the deputies wanted an account of the money raised for the wages of the muster master, officers and soldiers, and also for powder and match. The money paid by the Franchise of Bury is given in Tables 21 and 22.

In 1625 the Lord Lieutenant reported that the county was refusing to pay for a muster master.[57]

On 31 October 1627 the county's muster master, Captain Henry Woodhouse, was ordered to go to Plymouth to join the two newly raised regiments that were being sent to the Isle of Rhé. However his pay was in arrears so the Privy Council ordered the deputy lieutenants to collect the arrears and to send anyone who refused to pay before them.[58] In February 1628 the deputy lieutenants replied to the Privy Council's demand, and sent in a list of complaints from the people who were refusing to pay the arrears. The Privy Council was not pleased and reiterated their order to collect the arrears owing to Woodhouse and to bring before them anyone who refused to pay.[59] In May 1628 Woodhouse petitioned the Privy Council again, pointing that he had still not received any money, and that although he was not in the county he had left two able and sufficient deputies to fill his post.[60] Another letter to the deputy lieutenants followed on 15 July 1628.[61] By this time Captain Woodhouse's pay was two years in arrears. As far as the Privy Council knew, only one deputy lieutenant, Sir Thomas Jerman, had collected any money for Woodhouse and he was refusing to hand it over until the other deputy lieutenants had done the same. Once again the deputy lieutenants were told to gather the money and pay him or his deputy; they were to not make any excuses, nor accept, and to report anyone refusing to the Privy Council. The deputy lieutenants obviously felt strongly about

54 British Library, Add MS 39245, f.42.
55 British Library, Add MS 39245, f.71.
56 British Library Add MS 39245, ff.78–79.
57 4 Sep 1625, Audley End, Calendar of State Papers, Domestic, Vol. VI, p.97.
58 Lyle, *Acts of the Privy Council of England, 1627 September–1628 June*, p.112.
59 Lyle, *Acts of the Privy Council of England, 1627, Sept–1628 June*, p.322.
60 The National Archives, SP 16/105, f.199.
61 The National Archives, PC 2/38, f.295.

Table 21. Wages paid by the Franchise of Bury, 1624

For the two troops of horse under the command of Sir William Hervey;			
Hundred	£	s	d
Cosford	1	13	4
Babergh	3	6	8
Risbridge	2	10	0
Thedwestry	2	0	0
Blackbourn	2	10	0
Thingoe	1	13	4
Lackford	1	13	4
Bury St Edmunds	1	6	8
Total	16	13	8

Table 22. Wages paid by the Franchise of Bury, 1624

For the four foot companies in the Franchise of Bury;			
	£	s	d
Sir Robert Crane's Company			
Cosford Hundred	4	0	0
Twenty towns in Babergh Hundred	6	0	0
Sir George Le Hunt's Company			
Risbridge Hundred	8	0	0
Six towns in Babergh Hndred	2	0	0
Sir Thomas Jermyn's Company			
Thedwestry Hundred	3	12	0
Six towns in Babergh Hundred	1	8	0
Blackbourn Hundred	5	0	0
Sir John Heigham's Company			
Thingoe Hundred	3	6	8
Lackford Hundred	3	6	8
Bury St Edmunds	3	6	8
Totals	40	0	0

this issue as the arrears were not paid and no one was reported. The King intervened in this case and on 24 August 1628 he wrote to the deputies to inform them that although Captain Woodhouse was not present in the county, his duties would be carried out by an able deputy who should be paid and any arrears accrued from the last two years should also be paid.[62] The Privy Council wrote to the deputies again on 31 March 1629 repeating their previous demands that the money for Woodhouse be collected.[63] Despite the Council's displeasure the issue remained unresolved, and on 29 July 1629 the Council wrote to the deputies again, this time telling them that there were to be no excuses for not paying Captain Woodhouse his arrears of pay. They pointed out that although he had been absent from the county this had been at the express order of the King and that Woodhouse had left a capable deputy to carry on his duties. The deputy lieutenants were also told that his employment as the county's muster master was to continue and that they were to give him a list of dates and places of musters so that he could be present and do his duty.[64]

In February 1630, the town of Ipswich refused to pay towards the muster master's pay, previously they had raised £5 per year but due to increases in other taxes they could no longer afford this.[65] On 18 March the Privy Council wrote to the Lord Lieutenant in reply to a letter from his deputy lieutenants dated 19 January, concerning the muster master's pay,[66] which was now £100 per annum levied on the whole county. The Privy Council required the Lord Lieutenant and his deputies to order the high constables to collect this money, anyone refusing was to be reported to the Privy Council. They also informed the Lord Lieutenant that his deputies should in future show them more respect and act more promptly on their orders. In 1632 the muster master, Captain Woodhouse, was still owed money by the town of Ipswich which the Lord Lieutenant wanted paid.[67]

On 15 May 1632, Cratfield paid Mr Bedingfield £1 17s towards the pay arrears owed to the muster master;[68] later they paid another 9s 6d.

The Muster Master, Hampshire

In a letter dated 3 September 1627, the deputy lieutenants informed the Lord Lieutenant that they were having problems with a number of people refusing to pay towards the muster master's entertainment, especially a group in Winchester,[69] and the deputies wanted them to be dealt with sharply. A letter

62 The National Archives, Calendar of State Papers, Domestic Series, of the reign of Charles I, Mar 1628–June 1629, preserved in the State Paper Department of Her Majesty's Public Record Office. Vol. 3: Mar 1628–June 1629.

63 R.F. Monger (ed.), *Acts of the Privy Council of England*, Volume 44, 1628 July–1629 April (London: HMSO, 1958), p.379.

64 Dasent, *Acts of the Privy Council of England, 1629 May–1630 May*, p.107.

65 15 Feb 1630, Ipswich, Calendar of State Papers, Domestic Series, Vol. CLXI, p.188.

66 Dasent, *Acts of the Privy Council of England, 1629 May–1630 May*, p.316.

67 Suffolk Record Office, HD36/A/111.

68 Rev. William Holland, *Cratfield, a transcript of the accounts of the parish from 1490 to 1642, with notes* (London: Jarrold and Sons, 1895), p.167.

69 The National Archives, SP 16/76, f.26.

in Hampshire Record Office, undated but from about this time, gives a clue to the feeling of some of the county towards the costs of the muster master and other officials at the musters:[70]

> The Deputy Lieutenants or rather the Lord Lieutenant do appoint some of his servants or friends to be Muster Master & assign him a fee of £80 per annum for which he does nothing but adventure once a year at the time of musters he appears & shows himself busy about the examination of men's armour. His fee is laid by a common tax.
>
> This is not so where there be Commissioners of Musters, be it were fittest if need were of such a man to have one in the country by the choice of the J of P. This man might be had as well for £10 or 20 marks a year or for more.
>
> Then the Deputy Lieutenants have a clerk & he is the Lord Lieutenant's secretary & he keeps the books of musters & he challenges & takes off the constables of every town 12d for show of his common armour of the town.
>
> Then there is a stamp set upon every man's piece & a mark upon his arms for which they take fees and the pretence is to avoid borrowing of armour or muskets one of another. These fees make every [continues in the margin] year musters whereas they were wont to be seldom, the Deputy Lieutenants do give away rewards to captains that come to receive their soldiers as £20 or more & levy it upon the county without law.
>
> The Deputy Lieutenants take their charges of the country's money which was not want to be so & many more men are pressed than are needful or commanded & those and let go for fees and bribes of even to their men. And there is money levied for press, coat & conduct money of the country which ought not to be so.

---

70   Hampshire Record Office, 44M69/G5/36/15.

Open your   Charge

11

Take your charge in your right hand with the thumbe and fore finger thereof thrust of the cover.

5

The System and the Problems

The Muster System and the Men

Every county was expected to hold a general muster of the horse and foot at least once a year. Before the general muster there would be foot company and horse troop musters supervised by the captains with the assistance of the local deputy lieutenant and/or the county muster master, if required.

The methods used for mustering the foot and horse were different. For the foot these would initially be held to view the arms, armour and men to see if the arms and armour were serviceable and fit for purpose and the men were still alive and able to bear arms. This first foot company muster would then be followed by another muster, the time between the two being considered sufficient for any defects in the arms and armour to be repaired and for any gaps in the ranks of the soldiers to be filled with suitable men. The training of the soldiers would now begin, usually under the supervision of the captain but sometimes with the muster master present and possibly even a deputy lieutenant. The other people who may or may not have been summoned to these musters were those who provided the arms and armour. This category included the village constables, the clergy and ordinary men and women who either individually or collectively paid for arms and armour. Their presence was usually required at the viewings because these were the people who would have to pay for any repairs needed for the arms and armour and pay the soldiers their wages and expenses. Who attended the musters in addition to the soldiers was a matter for the Lord Lieutenant or his deputies.

The horse musters were very different from the foot musters. Most of the people who paid for the horsemen were wealthy and influential, and could not be ordered to appear before a mere captain or the muster master. Usually at least two deputy lieutenants were required and some input from the lord lieutenants was never refused.

The King and the Privy Council

At the top of the system was the King. Every year, in theory, he would order, or make his wishes known to, the Privy Council to issue the instructions for an annual muster of the trained band to be held in every county. The Privy Council would duly send out orders to the lord lieutenant(s) of each of the counties or to the commissioners for musters in those counties without a lord lieutenant. As well as the actual order for the muster, additional instructions could also be included, the order to replace calivers with muskets in 1618 being an example.[1] This was also the opportunity for the Privy Council to castigate those counties that had not sent in a muster certificate for the previous year or years.

The Lord Lieutenants

The post of lord lieutenant has been comprehensively written about a number of times and the present author would recommend *Noble Government, the Stuart Lord Lieutenancy and the Transformation of English Politics*, by Victor Slater, to those interested in this subject. When James I ascended to the throne, 16 counties did not have a lord lieutenant; by 1607 there were only four without one but slowly men were appointed in those counties, the last one being Nottinghamshire in 1626. The lord lieutenants of the counties were appointed by the King; a county could have more than one appointed and some men were the lord lieutenant of more than one county. The Lord Lieutenant of Wales controlled all of Wales and a varying number of English counties. The King could dismiss these men as he chose, but usually this was a position held until death. The lord lieutenants did not have to be resident in the county and some were often notable by their absence; they did have to have social standing in the county although this could be threatened if they fell into disfavour with the King. All were members of the nobility. When the lord lieutenant(s) received their orders from the Privy Council a letter would be sent to their deputies informing them of this order and often including a copy of the Privy Council's original letter. The letter to the deputies would usually include specific instructions that the lord lieutenant(s) thought needed emphasising and sometimes giving general dates for the musters. Some lord lieutenants who were resident within their county took a great interest in the trained bands; Leicestershire's Earl of Huntingdon actually wrote to the chief constables of each hundred and the Mayor of Leicester himself giving them their orders rather than leaving this to his deputies.[2]

---

1   John R. Dasent, *Acts of the Privy Council of England*, Volume 36, 1617–1619 (London: HMSO, 1933; reprint Nendeln/Lichtenstein: Kraus-Thomson Organization Ltd, 1974), pp.118–9.
2   Huntingdon Library, University of California, HA Military Box 1(17).

The Commissioners for Musters

The commissioners for musters were notable men within the county and would have been appointed by the Privy Council. The commissioners were the men who organised the musters in Elizabeth's reign and some continued in James'. On 21 August 1605 the King wrote to the Privy Council instructing them to supervise the musters in those counties where there was no lord lieutenant.[3] In 1614, four counties had commissioners for musters; these were Durham, Middlesex, Norfolk and Nottinghamshire.[4] In 1615 only Middlesex and Nottinghamshire still had commissioners for musters and this continued until 1622 when Middlesex acquired a lord lieutenant and deputy lieutenants. Nottinghamshire had to wait until 1626 for William Cavendish to be appointed its lord lieutenant. However in 1618 the Privy Council formed a commission for musters in Derbyshire,[5] where the post of lord lieutenant had become vacant, and this was filled in 1619. Many of these commissioners subsequently became deputy lieutenants.

The Deputy Lieutenants

At the start of James' reign all but eight counties in England and Wales had deputy lieutenants.[6] The men serving in those counties as deputies were local men of influence, initially appointed by the King or the Privy Council often at the same time as the lord lieutenant's appointment, though by 1625 all the lord lieutenants could appoint their own deputies. Before this time, the lord lieutenants were usually allowed a set number by the King. In 1615, when Lord Eure was about to be appointed Lord Lieutenant of Wales, he asked that each Welsh county be allowed to have four deputies and the English counties five or six.[7] Until 1617 the Privy Council appointed the deputy lieutenants for those counties which were under the jurisdiction of the Council of Wales;[8] in March 1617 this changed, and the Lord Lieutenant of Wales was permitted to appoint up to four deputies in each county. In November 1617 this changed again when the number that could be appointed was increased to six. From 1623 to 1625 the Privy Council resumed the responsibility for appointing deputy lieutenants, when this task was returned to the lord lieutenant. An example list of deputy lieutenants is included in Appendix VII; this list is for Yorkshire, the largest county.

The deputy lieutenants were local men and were required to be resident in the county although this was not always the case; the same group of men

---

3   Green, *Calendar of State Papers, Domestic Series, 1603–10*, p.231.

4   John R. Dasent, *Acts of the Privy Council of England*, Volume 33, 1613–1614 (Nendeln/Lichtenstein: Kraus-Thomson Organization Ltd, 1974), pp.552–6.

5   Dasent, *Acts of the Privy Council of England, 1617–1619*, p.116.

6   J.C. Sainty, 'Lieutenants of Counties, 1585–1642', *Bulletin of the Institute of Historical Research*, Special Supplement No. 8, May 1970, p.8.

7   The National Archives, SP 15/40.

8   J.C. Sainty, 'Lieutenants of Counties, 1585–1642', *Bulletin of the Institute of Historical Research*, Special Supplement No. 8, May 1970, pp.37–38.

were also Members of Parliament, Justices of the Peace and sheriffs. They had a number of tasks allocated to them including the trained bands, after the commissioners of musters were discontinued in those counties. When a muster took place, the attendance of at least two of them was required to sign off the muster certificate.[9] Many of these men had other roles, some being local such as being the colonel of a trained band regiment within their county, and other roles national, such as being a Member of Parliament (MP). Being an MP required the men to be in London at various times.

The deputy lieutenants would be written to by the lord lieutenants, who informed them of the requirement to hold a muster. A meeting would often then be arranged by the deputies to determine when and where the musters would be held and which of the deputy lieutenants would attend which musters. The efficiency of these men varied and sometimes they needed to be reminded of their duties. The Northamptonshire deputies were informed by their lord lieutenant in 1625 that the King was unhappy with them because they had not followed the instructions in the books that had been sent out to the counties;[10] in January 1626 the lord lieutenant informed them that he knew that these books had not been read and he was sending more, this time they were to sign to say that they had read them. In 1635 the Privy Council wrote to the Earl of Bridgwater regarding the annual musters in Wales, and the letter included a warning to the deputy lieutenants that the King was displeased with them regarding the musters over the last few years.[11] The Earl was required to rebuke all the deputies under his command.

The Justices of the Peace

Many of the deputy lieutenants were also Justices of the Peace (JPs); their authority was sometimes required when collecting money to pay for the musters and especially for the muster master. The support and the presence of the JPs who were not deputy lieutenants was also often expected at the musters.

The Captains

When a general muster was planned, the deputy lieutenants would send out a letter to each of the captains warning them of the date and place of the muster. In some counties a standard letter would be produced which then only required the captain's name and the date and place of the muster to be added, this was referred to as a "form of letters".

---

9   Historical Manuscripts Commission, *Twelfth Report, Appendix, Part I, The Manuscripts of the Earl Cowper, K.G.* (London: Eyre & Spottiswoode, 1888), p.412.
10   Bedfordshire Record Office J1289, dated 7 Sep 1625.
11   National Library of Wales, Wynn Paper, NLW MS9062E/1583.

The Head or Chief Constables

Each county was divided into a number of hundreds, wapentakes or rapes. A head constable was appointed to each of these, provided they were large enough, or one or more of them. These men were required to take an oath upon their appointment. An example can be found in Appendix II. The deputy lieutenants would send a warrant or precept to the head constables of each of the county's hundreds, wapentakes or rapes, instructing them to send similar warrants to the petty constables ordering them to bring the trained soldiers to the place of muster on the specified date, by a certain time. Sometimes they would also be ordered to bring along up to three suitable "supplies", these were men deemed suitable for service as a trained soldier in the place of a current soldier who was considered to be unfit for further service. The head constables were used to contact the petty constables to give them their written orders for the musters; there were usually two head or chief constables in each hundred, wapentake or rape within the counties.

The Petty Constables

Every village and town parish had at least one constable and sometimes two; the selected man or men usually served for a year, some of them had served in the trained band at other times. One of the main requirements for this role was that they could read and write. These men were required to attend the musters in most if not all the counties. If there was a problem with the soldier, arms or armour from their town, village or parish, then they were available to be told to correct these defects.

The Messengers

When a man was to be brought before the Privy Council it was not uncommon for a messenger to be sent to apprehend him. These messengers were messengers in name only; they appear to have had the power of arrest and seem to have held men in custody themselves, charging that man for the pleasure. The post could be, and was, abused. A good example of this is an incident that took place in Suffolk in 1635 with the Privy Council taking action on 9 June 1635, in response to Sir Richard Brooke reporting to the Council that on exercising his band of trained soldiers, five made default.[12] This absence was certified by the Lord Lieutenant of Suffolk, and messengers John Welch and Jasper Heily were sent to bring the men before "the Board". John Welch with the agreement of the deputy lieutenants and the captain discharged the defaulters, on their submission and promise of conformity, taking a very reasonable sum for his pains; however the other messenger, Jasper Heily, demanded and took £10 off two poor brothers, who were jointly

---

12   9 Dec 1635, Calendar of State Papers, Domestic Series, Vol. CCCIII, pp.546–7.

charged for a musket, which was a large amount for the two poor soldiers as well as being unlawful. He then discharged the two men without the permission of either a deputy lieutenant or the captain.

This was reported to the Privy Council and Jasper Heily was himself brought before it to answer the charges. The Council declared that:

> taking fees by messengers on the execution of warrants from the Board before the persons sent for have been heard before the Board, is a misdemeanour and exaction not to be suffered, unless in cases where the Lords shall express in the warrant, that the persons sent for shall be carried, in case of musters, either before the Lord Lieutenant of one of his deputies to be discharged, in which cases the messengers shall bring certificate of the discharge and of the fees received.

Heily was committed to the Fleet prison and was to give back the £10 he had taken before he could be released. The Lords also recommended the Lord Chamberlain suspend him, and the other messengers were to take notice of this case.

Local Government Versus Central Government

James and Charles, in London, knew what they wanted from the counties for the trained bands, just as the lord lieutenants and the deputy lieutenants in the counties knew what they were prepared and able to do to meet those requirements. Thus the musters were a source of disagreement between the central government and the local administration. Mustering the soldiers cost money and caused disruption, taking men away from their usual, daily employment. If musters had to be held, then the shorter they were, the better. Holding a muster and viewing the arms and armour meant that any defects were likely to be noted, if these meant that arms and armour had to be replaced then the costs would have to be borne by the local community, either as a whole for the common soldiers, or by individual people or groups of them, for the private soldiers. The musters were not popular. One way of avoiding this was to simply not hold one, which was very problematic, or simply not send in the muster return.

On 13 September 1614, as a result of the attack on Cleves by the Spanish Army, the Privy Council wrote to the lord lieutenants of all of the counties in England and Wales, the Lord Warden of the Stanneries and the Lord Warden of the Cinque Ports. The letter was an instruction to hold a general muster of the trained bands under their jurisdiction. They were to make sure that the bands were up to strength, all the officer posts were to be filled and the men were to be of the best quality; they were also to ensure that the county magazines were properly stocked.[13] The lord lieutenants of three counties responded to the Privy Council, and on 19 October the Privy Council wrote to the lord lieutenants of the "Middle Shires", Cumberland, Northumberland

---

13 Dasent, *Acts of the Privy Council of England*, 1613–1614, pp.552–6.

and Westmorland, concerning the recent instructions issued in September, on mustering the trained bands. These instructions caused a problem as it transpired that the "Middle Shires" had not been required to have a Trained Band. The Privy Council response was to order them to assess people so as to establish who could afford to pay for arms and equipment and then to raise men and form foot companies and horse troops. These were then to be mustered, viewed and trained from time to time.[14]

The 1614 muster returns from the counties that did return them were disappointing. On 26 June 1615 the Privy Council wrote to all the lord lieutenants expressing its concern with the state of the trained bands. They noted that the defects contained in the returns they had received were worrying, and assumed that those counties which had not submitted a return did so because their returns would have been even worse. The Council ordered that musters were to be held again and emphasised certain points. No one was exempt from this service any more – previously, the King's servants had been exempted but now were not – the clergy were to attend the musters with the laity, and the county magazines were to be properly stocked.[15]

On 30 April 1616 the Privy Council wrote to all of the lord lieutenants telling them that they were again still concerned about the state of the trained bands. Many counties had not submitted a muster return and those that did contained many defects, once again the Council assumed that those counties that did not submit a return did so because of the poor state of their soldiers. The lord lieutenants were ordered to hold a general muster and ensure that the trained bands were up to strength, that they were properly equipped, that the horse were properly mounted and armed, that the officers and soldiers were trained, that there were to be no exemptions, that the clergy were to be included and lastly that there was enough powder and munitions in the county magazines for the trained bands.[16]

As the county musters became a regular event the problems between the central government and the counties seemed to increase in number and intensity, and money was the still the biggest issue. It should be remembered that money was being raised in the counties for a number of separate purposes, not just for the trained bands. When money was raised locally and used locally for local needs there was less opposition to the levies being imposed, but where the money was being used for what the local people considered to be outside their county's control then there was opposition. The position of muster master was a cause of friction in most counties between local interests and the central government. The Privy Council sent frequent letters to various counties insisting that they pay their muster master's wages and the arrears that had accrued. The counties preferred prevarication and excuses to payment in most cases.

---

14 Dasent, *Acts of the Privy Council of England*, 1613–1614, pp.595–6.
15 Atkinson, E.G. (ed.), *Acts of the Privy Council of England*, Volume 34, 1615–1616 (Nendeln/ Lichtenstein: Kraus-Thomson Organization Ltd, 1974), pp.228–231.
16 Atkinson, E.G. (ed.), *Acts of the Privy Council of England*, Volume 34, 1615–1616 (Nendeln/ Lichtenstein: Kraus-Thomson Organization Ltd, 1974), pp.516–519.

The Money

Where did the money to pay for the trained band and its associated costs come from?

When James I came to the throne in 1603 the 1558 statute of Philip and Mary was in force. This laid down who was to be charged with providing certain types of arms and armour (see Chapter 1). In 1604 James repealed this statute but did not replace it with anything at that time. Following the repeal of the Philip and Mary statute many people believed that the Winchester Statutes of 1285 had come back into force, but in 1624 these too were repealed with nothing to replace them. Why James failed to replace them is not known, attempts were made in Parliament to do so but these came to nothing. As a result, the financing of the defence of this country came down to Royal Prerogative.

As a simple rule the money to pay for the private soldiers and their arms and armour came from individual wealthy citizens or small groups of them, the clergy, and in some towns the trade guilds. The money to pay for the common soldiers came from levies administered by the parish or village constables on the residents.

A number of problems existed with the various means of raising money. One was absentee landowners who would only pay in the parish or ward where they actually lived. This meant a shortfall in those parishes and wards where they owned land but refused to pay. The shortfall had to be covered by the remaining residents, and this was deemed to be unfair. Another issue was that of parish arms: all parishioners were supposed to pay except those already paying for private arms. However, in a number of counties the lord lieutenants had ordered that all residents should pay for them, regardless.[17] Having to pay twice caused some resentment.

Two towns in Shropshire, Shrewsbury and Ludlow, used different systems to provide the soldiers required for the trained band. Shrewsbury provided 39 soldiers; the trade guilds of the town provided numbers of both pikemen, musketeers and targeteers.[18] How these allocations were decided upon is not known but the numbers for 1622 and 1626 are shown in Table 23. As can be seen, the number of men provided by the trade guilds dropped from 25 in 1622 to 16 in 1626, the two targets previously provided are gone and the number of muskets dropped by over half. The rest of its trained soldiers were common soldiers provided by parishes within the town.

Ludlow provided 24 soldiers for the trained band; all were private soldiers and each of them was paid for by between one and five individuals.[19] These men and women, or finders, were responsible for different aspects of the financing of a soldier. In some cases they seemed to have pooled their money,

---

17 Peter Clark, Alan Smith, Nicholas Tyacke (eds), *The English Commonwealth 1547–1640*, Chapter 5, 'Militia Rates and Militia Statutes, 1558–1663', A Hassell-Smith (Leicester: Leicester University Press, 1979).

18 Shropshire Archives 3365/2563.

19 Shropshire Archives LB7/2181.

whereas in others they assumed the cost for one or more items, his pay, or his expenses when he was training.

Table 23. Trade guild troop allocations, Shrewsbury and Ludlow

Trade Guild	Musket		Corslet		Target
	1622	1626	1622	1626	1622
Drapers			2	2	
Mercers	1	1	1	1	
Shermen			1		1
Corvisors			1	2	1
Weavers	1		1		
Bakers	1	1			
Tailors			1	1	
Glovers	1	1	1		
Butchers	1	1			
Carpenters & Tilers	1		1	1	
Fletchers, Boyers, Coopers & Joiners	1				
Saddlers & Painters	1		1	1	
Smiths	1				
Tanners	1		1	1	
Barbers	1	1			
Cloth workers	1			2	
	12	5	11	11	2

The Clergy

Charging the clergy with providing arms and armour was always problematic. The Archbishop of Canterbury decided which clergymen would be charged with providing arms and armour; he consulted with his bishops, and once an agreement had been reached the names of those clergymen who were to provide arms and armour would be sent to the deputy lieutenants. The deputies had no involvement in these decisions.

In a letter from the Archbishop of Lincoln to Sir John Lambe at Peterborough, sent on 30 June 1615, the Archbishop wanted copies of the old books held there, presumably the muster books showing what specific, individual clergymen had paid for on previous occasions.[20] He also wanted to know the current value of the parishes that the clergymen currently held.

---

20   The National Archives, SP 14/80, f.194.

The Archbishop told Sir John that the following rates were to be used to assess what the clergymen should be charged with:

Below £40 p.a., nothing
£40–£50 p.a., two men to be put together to buy a musket
£60 p.a., two to be put together to buy a corslet
£70–£100 p.a., a musket
£100–£140 p.a., a corslet
£140–£200 p.a., a petronel
Over £200 p.a., a lance

On 6 August 1635, a table listing the obligations of Kent's clergy was produced.[21] The document also listed the arms, armour and men that had been sent by the clergy to the musters in Kent in previous years. These obligations had been approved by the Archbishop of Canterbury. The agreement was that those clergymen with livings worth under £20 did not provide anything, although they could be banded together with other clergymen so as to be able to provide something. Those with living worth £40 or more were to provide a corslet, £60 or more a musketeer, £80 to £100 a musketeer and a corslet, £130 or more a light horseman, £150 or more a light horseman and a corslet and those with a living worth more than £160, a light horseman and a musketeer. These assessments had enabled the clergy to provide 23 light horsemen, 107 musketeers and 101 corslets in 1634 and 18 light horsemen, 106 musketeers and 66 corslets in 1633.

The system used by many villages was a levy on all those who had money or property. The constable of the village of Wymeswold in Leicestershire noted in his accounts, "Another levy made upon the 17 day of October 1605, for money which the Constable of Wymeswold has laid forth in showing the armour and such like. Every 20 acres of land, 4d, and the cottagers, a penny a beast."[22] The village of Edmondthorpe also used levies to raise money to pay its costs.[23] From 1635 to 1638 the village was charged at 1d an acre and from 1639 2d an acre.

At the 1615 Hampshire sessions, eight of the justices ordered that a levy should be imposed on the county to pay the county's muster master, Captain Robert Goswell, his annual pay of £80.[24] This was to be raised by divisions as shown in Table 24.

The Justices were to write to the constables of each hundred, the rate used was to be the same as that used for "other levies for other collections" which were not specified. Of the eight Justices, three were also deputy lieutenants and another two were officers in the trained band.

The Justice for the Andover Division apportioned the following amounts to the parishes within his division as shown in Table 25.

---

21 The National Archives, SP 16/295, f. 92.
22 British Library Add MS 10457, f.7.
23 Leicester Record Office, DE670/14.
24 Hampshire Record Office, 4M53/140, ff.82–84.

Table 24. Levy on Hampshire divisions, 1615

Division	Amount
Alton	£12 0s 0d
Andover	£12 0s 0d
Basingstoke	£12 12s 0d
Fawley	£12 0s 0d
Kingsclere	£9 4s 0d
New Forest	£12 0s 0d
Portsdown	£9 4s 0d

Table 25. Andover Division, amounts apportioned to parishes

Parish	Amount
Andover Extra	£2 13s 4d
Andover Intra	£1 6s 8d
Barton Stacey	£1 16s 8d
Kings Sombourne	£2 13s 4d
Thorngate	£2 13s 4d
Wherwell	£1 6s 8d

The levy for the Parish of Thorngate was also broken down into contributions from the 10 individual villages within it.

On 23 September 1605 the Deputy Lieutenants of Norfolk met at the King's Head in Norwich to decide a rate for the provision of the trained band.[25] This was needed due to the repeal of the statute of Philip and Mary for the finding of arms and armour. The rate agreed upon by the deputy lieutenants was as follows:[26]

Estates of £200 per annum in land or £2,000 in goods to provide a corslet, a musket, both furnished and a lance.

Estates of 100 marks per annum or 1,000 marks in goods to provide a light horse and one foot armour.

Estates of £40 per annum or £500 in goods to provide a petronel and a foot armour.

Estates of £15 per annum or £200 in goods to provide a musket or a corslet, both furnished.

Estates of £10 per annum or 200 marks in goods to provide a caliver.

---

25 British Library King's MS 265, f.618.

26 Victor Morgan, Elizabeth Rutledge, Barry Taylor (eds), *The Papers of Nathaniel Bacon of Stiffkey*, Vol. V, 1603–07 (Norwich: Norfolk Record Society, 2010), pp.209–210.

The local captain was to decide in those cases whether the foot armour was to be a musketeer or a pikeman.

The musters were paid for by levies in the towns and villages where those who could pay were required to pay a certain rate according to their means. There were problems on occasion, such as in Woodhouse Eaves in Leicestershire in May 1616, when two men from the village had action taken against them for refusing to pay towards the costs of the trained bands and the King's household.[27] Later, in an undated letter but probably pre-Civil War, the village constable and a number of other men wrote to the lord lieutenant regarding one man who was refusing to pay despite being considered wealthy.[28]

---

27 Leicester Record Office, DG9/2269-70.
28 Leicester Record Office, DG9/2272.

Charge   with Bullet

13

Take the Bullet forth of your bag
or out of your mouth and put it
into the muzell of your Musket

6

Effectiveness

Were the trained bands an effective force? The answer depends on what their function was intended to be.

The trained bands had at least two functions: one was national defence and the other a mix of public order and internal security. During the first half of James' reign it was perceived that no current external threat existed but there were still internal disturbances for the trained band to deal with. This encouraged a more relaxed view of the trained bands' functions.

The Privy Council wrote to the Lord Lieutenant of Derbyshire on 30 June 1605 to tell him to order the county to hold a muster and view twice a year; the men and their arms and armour were to be viewed but not trained.[1] The main necessity was to view the arms and armour, which could be done at convenient times and places. Training could be relaxed due to there being no current threat to the realm. This letter was a standard letter sent to all the counties.

In that same year, 1605, the Gunpowder Plot took place. Worcestershire Trained Band soldiers were probably involved in the hunting down of the plotters and were present at the taking of the plotters at Holbeach on 8 November. The relaxed view of the trained band taken by the Government probably ended about then.

In 1607 there were serious disturbances in the Midlands caused by the enclosure of land. During June 1607 Sir Thomas Cave, one of the deputy lieutenants of Leicestershire, ordered that 40 armed men be mustered and trained on that day and the next in Leicester.[2] These men were to be used to suppress a number of disorderly people who were tearing down hedges on enclosed ground in the area of Welland in the south of the county. These 40 men do not appear to have been members of the trained band; they were referred to as "harness men" and were paid a total of 21s. The Earl of Shrewsbury, the Lord Lieutenant of Derbyshire, wrote to his deputy lieutenants on 2 June 1607 to tell them what had been happening in the county of Northamptonshire during the enclosure riots. He told them that

---

1   Lambeth Palace Archives, Talbot Papers, f.382.
2   Leicestershire Record Office, BRIII/2/75 1606–10, p.31/

Sir Anthony Mildmay and Sir Edward Montagu had gone to Newton and found a 1,000-strong group of rioters. The local trained band had proved reluctant to take action against these men, so the two deputy lieutenants had been obliged to arm their own tenants and servants and had then attacked the rioters, killing 40 or 50 of them.[3]

On 4 November 1613 William James, the Bishop of Durham, wrote to the Privy Council regarding the required muster and view of the county's trained band.[4] He informed the Council that he had acquainted the JPs with its requirement for the county, and these had fulfilled. He noted that the county had previously been required to maintain 400 trained men and 400 untrained men made up of 400 corslets and 400 shot, and informed the Privy Council that few of them were good but were in readiness. Neither the corslets nor the shot were fit for current service, having been bought for use in the last rebellion and in 1588, and been poorly kept since then. The Justices, the gentlemen and other wealthy men wanted to buy the new equipment now so that they would not have to pay out again for some time. The Bishop now wanted to know what proportion of the men should be pikemen and how many musketeers, the ratio of 33 or 35 corslets to 100 shot they thought may mean too few pikes, but this was the ratio used in other counties. However it was pointed out that Durham, being a coastal county and having many havens and creeks, needed more shot and fewer pikes. What was the Privy Council's wish? As for the horse, the Bishop said the clergy and the gentlemen would raise 50 light horse in the county and if the Middle Shires, Cumberland, Northumberland and Westmorland, did the same then a good-sized force would be available when combined. Finally, there was feeling among many in the county that they should dispense with 100 of the untrained foot and retain 100 light northern horsemen instead, and this could also apply to the Middle Shires. These men would be better and more useful than the usual light horsemen.

The lack of a perceived external threat to the country was now due to change. With that change the need for the trained bands to be ready to repel an external enemy came to the fore.

On 26 June 1615 the Privy Council wrote two letters; one, to the lord lieutenants and commissioners of musters, concerning the poor state of the trained bands, has already been noted. The second was sent to the Archbishops of Canterbury and York to tell them that the King required their clergymen to provide horses, arms and armour to the trained bands.[5] The Archbishops were required to write to their bishops, who in turn were to provide lists of their clergymen who were already charged with providing arms and armour and in addition adding the names of those not already charged who could afford to pay. Both resident and non-resident clergy were to be included. These lists were to be sent to the lord lieutenants and

---

3   A Calendar of the Talbot Papers, vol. M, p.285, f.401.
4   The National Archives, SP 14/75, f.1.
5   The National Archives, PC 2/28, f.25.

commissioners for musters of the counties under their jurisdiction. By 30 June the Archbishops' letters were being sent out to their bishops.[6]

At this point a different perspective of the trained bands might be useful. The Venetian Ambassador in 1622 wrote a report on the martial abilities of the country, and this gives two opinions.[7] The first is his opinion of the potential of the country based on those men fighting in the Low Countries, and the second is his view of the trained band, horse and foot, and the fighting spirit in the country. Whilst he undoubtedly had opportunities to see the London Trained Bands and possibly those of the surrounding counties, it is unlikely that he ventured very far from London.

He noted that every man was obliged to serve if the country was invaded, and believed that every town and county had paid captains and that the men were armed and ready for war. As proof of this he quoted the Prince of Orange whose opinion of the men from this country fighting for him was that there were no better soldiers once they had got over the initial hardships. They were determined in battle and feared death less than other men. However, he believed that James had pacified the country to the extent that the natural military spirit of many men had disappeared.

The Ambassador also gave his opinion on the quality of the trained bands. The cavalry was not well thought of and he noted that there were no cavalry units abroad. The cavalry were mostly lightly armed with a few equipped as lancers or cuirassiers. The horses, he thought, were numerous but these were only good for speed and pleasure; there were some heavy horses in Cornwall but they were of no military use, and no more than 400 of them. The horsemen did not like discomfort but loved pleasure and convenience and he thought they made better huntsmen than soldiers. He did not believe that more than 3,000 or 4,000 ill-armed and ill-disciplined cavalry could be brought together in a crisis. His thoughts on the foot were also very telling: he thought the captains and the men only served for appearance and not use, and cared for little else other than eating, drinking and smoking tobacco in the taverns. The musters were attended more for sport and pleasure than for serious training. He believed that out of every 1,000 men, only 100 knew how to use a pike or musket and even they were not very good. He also noted that there were usually 13,000 to 14,000 men serving in the Low Countries, where those likely to be a nuisance were sent.

The troops pressed for the Mansfeld expedition caused problems in Essex. As a result, in December 1624 the Privy Council ordered the Essex deputy lieutenants to use the trained band to maintain order among the pressed men.[8]

On 1 February 1627 the Privy Council wrote to the Lord Mayor of London and the deputy lieutenants of Middlesex, concerning the possibility of disturbances on Shrove Tuesday. The Mayor was to have at least 200 men

---

6   The National Archives, SP 14/80, f.196.
7   Allen B. Hinds, *Calendar of State Papers and Manuscripts, Relating to English Affairs, Existing in the Archives and Collections of Venice*, Vol. XVII, 1621–1623 (London: The Hereford Times Limited, 1911), pp.432–433.
8   Dasent, *Acts of the Privy Council of England*, 1623–1625, pp.407, 409–410.

from the trained band mustered at points where they could quickly intervene if trouble broke out.[9]

Another letter was sent from the Privy Council to the Lord Mayor and Court of Aldermen of London on 16 February 1627. The Sheriffs had complained to them of the insolencies and disorders committed daily upon inhabitants of the city by mariners and other loose persons. The Privy Council wanted a sufficient number of the trained bands to be armed and in readiness to disperse any such tumultuous assemblies, and in the event of resistance to assail and disperse them in hostile manner as rebels. Further, strong and sufficient watches should be kept both day and night at the gates and other usual places in the city, for the prevention of tumults and disorders.[10] These disorders seem to have occurred on an almost annual basis in London during this period.

The Privy Council also sent a letter to all the lord lieutenants of a number of the counties on 31 May 1628,[11] stating that due to the current problems in Christendom, every man should be ready to defend it. The King had intended to inspect the horse from a number of counties at Hounslow in the summer but due to the expected expenses that muster had been cancelled. The Privy Council noted that previously there had been too much neglect in many counties and the King wanted all defects rectified for the musters which were now to be held in each county. All muster certificates were to be returned by 10 September and a list of those counties failing to so would be given to the King. This letter does indicate that as far as the King and the Privy Council were concerned, the trained bands were defective by reason of a lack of muster certificates being sent to London. These counties were Bedfordshire, Cumberland, Essex, Hertfordshire, Huntingdonshire, Leicestershire, Lincolnshire, Norfolk, Northamptonshire, Northumberland, Nottinghamshire, Rutland, Westmorland, and Yorkshire.

On 14 February 1629, in a letter to the Warden of the Cinque Ports, the Privy Council referred to a large riot in Fleet Street in London that required the trained band to be used to suppress it.[12] This incident caused the Council to tell the Lord Mayor that the trained band had proved unequal to the task when this riot occurred, and the reason was that the musketeers had no powder or shot available to them. The Council ordered that every soldier was now to have powder and shot available in their homes, ready for use.[13]

In 1629, probably on 30 April, the Privy Council wrote to all the lord lieutenants regarding the trained band musters which they believed had been neglected;[14] the King was aware of the situation and was very displeased. The lord lieutenants were ordered to hold exact views of the trained band, horse

---

9   J.V. Lyle (ed.), *Acts of the Privy Council of England*, Volume 42, 1627 January–August (London: HMSO, 1938), p.47.

10 H.C. Overall and W.H. Overall, *Analytical index to the series of records known as the Remembrancia: preserved among the archives of the City of London, A.D. 1579–1664* (London: E.J. Francis, 1878), VI, 141, pp.534–535.

11 The National Archives, PC 2/38 f.185.

12 Dasent, *Acts of the Privy Council of England, 1629 May–1630 May*, p.83.

13 Dasent, *Acts of the Privy Council of England, 1629 May–1630 May*, p.126.

14 The National Archives, PC 2/39, f.227.

and foot, at a convenient time following receipt of the letter. The soldiers were to be equipped in a modern fashion and were to be trained either by the Low Countries sergeants and officers or by some other experienced person. The officers were also to be trained in the performance of their duties, appropriate to their rank. The soldiers, officers and men were to be physically able and "sufficient", and well-affected in religion. All were to take the oaths of Supremacy and Allegiance. No man was to leave his place of residence without permission from the local deputy lieutenant, and if a man did leave then another man was to take his place, thereby maintaining the trained band's strength. They were also to ensure that any properties that formerly were charged with providing arms and armour but had changed ownership were once again charged. A note was included as to which counties had made a muster return in 1628. Table 26 below shows which counties made a return and those which did not:

Some observations should be made here regarding the returning of a muster certificate. If a county held a muster and it went well, those responsible for the muster would submit a return. If the muster did not go well, they might submit a return, or send in a letter delaying their return until the problems were rectified, or not submit a return. If the muster went badly or did not take place then no return would be submitted and all letters requesting a return would be ignored. The latter course was taken because the consequences of sending in a bad return were greater than not sending in a return. The worse that could happen if no return was sent in was a letter of chastisement for it. If a bad return was sent in then the lord lieutenants and deputies could be summoned before the Privy Council. The Council was well aware of all this and would occasionally threaten to summon the lord lieutenants and their deputies to London if no return was made on time. This threat was made in 1628 but there is no record of it being carried out. Also, the instances where counties reportedly did or did not send in a return should be noted. Musters were held in Somerset in late 1628 and there were problems of which the Privy Council were aware, but the county evidently did not submit a return. There is no evidence of musters being held in Wiltshire in 1628, so the report of no return is probably correct. Suffolk reportedly did not submit a return. The musters were actually held in Suffolk in that year, as the accounts of the constable of Cratfield show money spent on sending its nine soldiers to the muster and money spent on powder and match.[15] The three Middle Shires of Cumberland, Northumberland and Westmorland did not submit returns but their lord lieutenants responded to this by pointing out that they were still trying to raise men to fill the ranks, so holding musters was not yet an option; this was 14 years after being ordered to do so.

As a final point, just over half of the counties submitted a return for 1628. Some of those that were reported as failing to do this did hold musters but chose not to send in a return for whatever reason. This does show that the trained bands were not being neglected, as Charles and the Privy Council thought. It does show that some counties were encountering serious problems, however.

---

15 Holland, *Cratfield, a transcript of the accounts of the parish*, p.163.

Table 26. County muster returns, 1628

No return made	Return made
Berkshire	Anglesey
Buckinghamshire	Bedfordshire
Brecknock	Cambridgeshire
Cumberland	Cardigan
Denbigh	Carmarthen
Durham	Carnarvon
Essex	Cheshire
Flint	Cinque Ports
Glamorgan	Cornwall
Kent	Derbyshire
Lincoln	Devonshire
Merioneth	Dorset
Middlesex	Gloucestershire
Montgomery	Hampshire
Northumberland	Herefordshire
Shropshire	Hertfordshire
Somerset	Huntingdonshire
Staffordshire	Lancashire
Suffolk	Leicestershire
Sussex	Monmouth
Warwickshire	Norfolk
Westmorland	Northamptonshire
Wiltshire	Nottinghamshire
Worcestershire	Oxfordshire
Yorkshire	Pembroke
	Radnor
	Rutland
	Surrey
Total: 25	Total: 28

Sir Edward Bayntun of Wiltshire was elected as an MP seven times between 1614 and 1640, was serving as a deputy lieutenant by 1626 and continued to serve until at least 1631. In 1626 he was also the colonel of a regiment of trained band horse. In 1631 he was ordered by the Sheriff of Wiltshire to muster at Warminster with 100 pikes and muskets to help evict some farmers from Selwood Forest. Despite being a deputy lieutenant, Bayntun refused, saying that "he did not much fancy that work". He sided with Parliament at the start of the Civil War.[16]

On 5 April 1631 the Privy Council wrote to the Lord Lieutenant of Gloucestershire, a Justice of the Peace and the Sheriff, ordering them to ready the trained band. This was due to a disturbance in the Forest of Dean where a mob of about 500 people had gathered and begun filling in ditches, closing off coal pits and attacking a local man's house. The Privy Council was worried about the disturbance spreading.[17] Later, on 8 April, the mob was reported to be 1,000 strong and was now reported as being rebellious. The Lord Lieutenant was now ordered to prepare the deputy lieutenants and the trained band for the suppression of the mob.[18] Matters did not proceed as the Privy Council had hoped, and on 22 June they wrote to the Deputy Lieutenants, Sheriff and Justices of the Peace accusing them of disrespecting the King. They were ordered to do their duty including their use of the trained band and send reports of their actions to the Privy Council. Letters on this matter were also sent to the Lord Lieutenant and the Chief Justice of the Marches of Wales.[19]

The effectiveness of the Yorkshire Trained Band in 1637 might be gauged with an example from 1637. Sir Hugh Cholmley, a deputy lieutenant, noted an incident when two Dutch ships chased a smaller Spanish vessel into the port of Whitby in the North Riding.[20] The incident required Sir Hugh to call out the local trained band to thwart the Dutch attempt to take the Spanish

---

16 <http://www.historyofparliamentonline.org/volume/1604-1629/member/bayntun-sir-edward-1593-1657>, accessed 14 February 2017.

17 Dasent, *Acts of the Privy Council of England, 1630 June–1631 June*, pp.284–5.

18 Dasent, *Acts of the Privy Council of England, 1630 June–1631 June*, pp.289–290.

19 Dasent, *Acts of the Privy Council of England, 1630 June–1631 June*, pp.390–1.

20 Jack Binns (ed.), *The Memoirs and Memorials of Sir Hugh Cholmley of Whitby, 1600–57* (Woodbridge: Yorkshire Archaeological Society, 2000), pp.96–98.

ship. He lamented that of the 200 men on guard only a few of them, seamen, knew how to handle their weapons or fire a musket.

The Lord Lieutenant of Cambridgeshire wrote to his deputies on 23 November 1638 including a copy of the Privy Council's letter.[21] He noted that despite the many letters sent, the deputies had seldom sent in a return for the musters. He also doubted that some of the men in the trained band knew how to use their weapons, so they would fail in a battle. The deputies were ordered to call a muster and return an exact certificate to the Lord Lieutenant, and they duly wrote to the captains on 1 December with orders for the musters. In their letter the captains were told of the requirement to have their companies at a day's notice to move and that their men were to be instructed and trained in the use of their weapons either by the muster master or another experienced officer, whom they were not to choose. The men could be mustered and trained in small groups but there was to be a company muster in December which the deputies would be attending. The efforts of the deputies towards the horse troop did not escape the Privy Council's notice. On 31 December the Lord Lieutenant wrote to the deputies informing them that they should have returned a number of men as defaulters but instead did nothing. Their certificate was also late in arriving; this was not to happen again.

The trained bands were also intended to be used to garrison certain strongpoints on the coast. In Hampshire a foot company was allocated to reinforce the garrison of Hurst Castle, while in Cornwall four foot companies were allocated to the defence of Pendennis Castle.[22] The company allocated to Hurst Castle was armed entirely with muskets while the four companies earmarked for Pendennis were a mix of pikes and muskets; in 1627 there were 235 muskets and 161 pikemen, a total of 396 soldiers, in 1628 the numbers were 236 muskets and 158 pikemen giving a total of 394 soldiers. The parallel figures for Cornwall give ratios of musket to pike of 59 percent to 41 percent for 1627 and 60 percent to 40 percent for 1628, which are about the national average.

So were the trained bands an effective force? As an internal security force they seem to have been ineffective. One of the reasons for that may have been their reluctance to act against their neighbours and people with whom they may have sympathised. As a force to counter an external threat they do not inspire great confidence, and yet the Venetian Ambassador was impressed by the "raw material", and British soldiers did perform well on the Continent. It is the present author's opinion that given the right circumstances they could have done what was required of them; fighting for their homes and families, side by side with their friends and neighbours, they would have fought, and fought hard. Ask them to do something they did not believe in however, and they were reluctant to act.

---

21 British Library, Harley MS 4014, ff.26–30.
22 The National Archives, SP 16/72, f.19, and SP 16/259, f.11.

Draw forth y^r scou ring stick

14

With your right hand (y^t Palme turned from you) draw forth your scouring stick bearing your bodie and y^r left hand $w^{th} y^e$ Musket soe farrbacke as you can

7

Uniforms, Ribbons and Colours

Uniforms

There is very little information available regarding the uniforms, if there were any, of the trained bands in this period. There are very few references to money being paid out for clothing for the trained band soldiers and almost all of these are in James' reign. Those men pressed for service had their clothing paid for but not, it would appear, the trained soldiers, at least not in Charles' reign. The foremost army in Europe, that of the Spanish, does not appear to have had uniforms in unit colours at this time, the requirement being merely that the clothes supplied were of the same pattern.[1]

There are a few hints and clues to some aspects of trained band uniform, mostly for the horse. In a Devon document dated to 1586 it was noted that "Justices that are not of the quorum, one petronel, one ordinary gelding, to attend upon the Lieutenant to be clad in cassocks of one colour at the charges of the said Justices."[2] Whilst predating the period being written about here, it is possible that these details remained the same into at least the early part of James' reign.

Similarly, in Essex an order was issued for the uniforms of the county's light horsemen; the document is undated but probably dates to the late 1590s, again a little before the period considered here, but the order quite possibly ran into the early seventeenth century. The order required that the furniture of every light horse was to consist of "a light northern sadle, a simple hedstall, reynes and pettrell with a strap and socket for the staff". The rider's armour was to be "a coat of plate, fitted to his bodie ... a red capp and a skull, an arming sword, dagger and a girdle ... pistols." The rider's clothing was to be "a liverye cassock of brodecloth of friers graie made close before, and open on

---

1   Geoffrey Parker, *The Army of Flanders and the Spanish Road, 1567–1659* (Cambridge: Cambridge University Press, 1972), pp.164–5.
2   Devon Heritage Centre, 3799M-3-O-2-4.

every side, and garded with two verie narrowe gardes of cloth, the one blewe, the other yellow".[3]

In Surrey it is known that the two soldiers provided through the Lambeth churchwardens wore red coats between at least 1599 and 1610.[4] The coats were made in 1599 and for both coats six yards of red cloth were used which cost 2s 2d per yard; also used were "4 dozen of white tape and white thread" which cost another 18d. The tailor, Frances Heyd, was paid 2s 8d. An inventory taken in 1610 of the church armoury included two red soldiers' coats. In 1614 10s was paid for two new soldiers coats but no colour was mentioned. Whether the rest of the county wore uniforms is not known.

During 1616 a muster was held at Great Torrington in the North Division of Devon, and the soldiers from the Borough of Hartland attended this muster.[5] The costs incurred by the borough included 4s 10d for a new coat for one of the pikeman, which was to be worn under the armour. The records do not give any colours or any other details but it is one of the few mentions of coats being supplied to the trained soldiers.

Badges of rank were not always made of material. The muster return for Pevensey, one of the Cinque Ports, dated 1 April 1619, includes the names of the officers and the numbers of men in the trained band.[6] The officers included Captain Edward Millward, Lieutenant John Millward, Ensign John Caslreat, Corporal Thomas Stroker and Drummer Christopher Caslreat. These four men, less the drummer, were equipped with a pair of curats and a halberd each, distinguishing them from the rank and file.

A letter was sent from Sir Edmond Mundford to Sir William de Grey, a deputy lieutenant and commander of the foot company in Wayland Hundred, Norfolk in June 1621.[7] Sir Edmond informed Sir William that he was sending his two pikemen to the company muster but noted:

> I have sent to your muster two pikemen wherewith I am charged, I have sent them only with their pikes, headpieces, gorgets, coats and swords and daggers in regard of the uncertainty of the winter weather, the armour is all ready and full furnished, and if you think it requisite to have it when you train, it shall be there, but if it may be spared I shall thankfully accept thereof, I know not with what colour you will have your pikes armed and therefore have left them bare until I hear from you, my light horse and man I have also sent with coat, staff, pistol, gorget and headpiece.

For the pikemen and the horsemen a coat is included in their list of equipment, possibly indicating a uniform coat. The fact that it is part of the equipment provided indicates that it was not a personal item of wear provided by the soldier in either case.

---

3   Essex Record Office, D/Y 2/3, p.86.
4   Lambeth Church Wardens Books 1504–1645, book i. p.210 and book ii. pp.233, 273.
5   Ivon L. Gregory (ed.), *The Hartland Church Accounts 1597–1706* (Frome: Butler & Tanner, 1950), pp.76–78.
6   The National Archives, SP 14/108, f.9.
7   Norfolk Record Office, WLS XVII/2,410X5.

In 1628 Bristol Corporation paid Robert Elliott £3 13s 3d for 9¾ yards of fine red cloth for suits for the drummers in Captain Taylor's company, and paid another £2 16s for six dozen, presumably yards, of black and white silk ribbon for the drummers.[8] The question then is, if the drummers are dressed in red were the rest of the company also wearing red? Also since there is no mention of the Corporation paying for any material, if the men were uniformed, who paid for it?

At a muster was held in Middlesex on 18 June 1635,[9] the captains raised a number of issues with the deputy lieutenants. The captains of the foot companies were complaining about the amount of money they had to pay their officers, sergeants, corporals and drummers at the musters, and the soldiers in their turn were also complaining about the cost of their apparel and arms, indicating that their clothing was possibly of a uniform type, specific to the musters and provided by the soldiers themselves.

An order issued by the Council of War in 1635 included a note regarding the cuirassiers appearance.[10] This read:

> no cuirassier shall carry either feather or coat, but scarf of rich crimson taffeta, according as is now used in the War, which is to be two ells (1 ell equalled 5 feet) in length cut through the breadth at 15d a piece and buying a whole piece together, they will be so much the cheaper, and the charge will prove less than that of coats and feathers and will be more serviceable and soldier like and will last longer.

To me this indicates that those horsemen equipped as cuirassiers were no longer issued with a coat. The sash or scarf was now providing the uniform element for the cuirassier.

Ribbons

One other method of identifying soldiers' companies appears to have been the use of ribbons. These are mentioned a number of times in the accounts of a number of towns in different counties and in the accounts for the musters.

For the Leicestershire county muster in 1615, the Lord Lieutenant informed the Mayor of Leicester that the men selected to serve as the town's soldiers had to be mustered on 12 October, by nine o'clock.[11] Leicester Corporation paid for 44 yards of white ribbon and another 44 yards of "watched" ribbon, no colour specified. The white ribbon cost 6d per yard, the cost of the other ribbon is not known but the overall cost was £2. This was given to the town's soldiers as favours to distinguish them from the rest of the trained band, and it was noted that every captain had his own colour.

---

8   D.M. Livock, *City chamberlains' accounts in the sixteenth and seventeenth centuries* (Bristol: Bristol Record Society, 1966), Vol. XXIV, pp.108–9.

9   The National Archives, SP 16/312, f.128.

10 Rye, *State papers relating to musters*, p.202.

11 Leicestershire Record Office, Records of the Borough of Leicester, BR/II/18/12, f.2.

Leicester's Corporation also paid 3s for 2 yards of "Levin" taffeta, no colour mentioned (probably from the Levant), for a drummer, Thomas Nurce, to lead their soldiers out to the captain.[12]

Similarly in Nottingham on 6 September 1616 Nottingham town council decided to muster its soldiers on the following Monday at eight o'clock.[13] An additional cost for the muster was a payment of 4s for ribbons for the 16 common soldiers of the town.[14] No actual colours for the town were mentioned.

In May 1627 Nottingham bought 26 yards of ribbon for its 16 common soldiers, this cost 5d per yard, the total cost was 10s 10d.[15] This gives a total of 26 yards of ribbon for 16 men, about five feet of ribbon per man.

The two Derbyshire foot companies were issued with ribbons in 1635; these were issued to every trained soldier at a cost of 1s for each soldier, a total of £20 being expended. The ribbons were noted as being in the respective captain's colour.[16] This would seem to indicate that the captains used a single colour each.

In January 1639, Gravesend paid for a new corslet costing £1 15s and 1s for powder and ribbon for its musketeer.[17] Whether this was actually ribbon as part of the uniform or match for the musket cannot be ascertained.

Colours

The word colour in this study has two distinct meanings. The company flag was a colour and is referred to as "the colours". The second meaning refers to the captains' colours. These were used on the pike shafts of the company that the captain commanded. When these colours were applied, the pike was then referred to as being armed, if it did not have the colours on it then it was bare or unarmed. There is more information on pike colouring than flags, so pikes will be looked at first.

In the Twysden lieutenancy papers for Kent, there is an account for April 1591 that lists the cost for the equipping of a pikeman, and among the various costs is an entry that reads "For the arminge of each pike with the Captain's colour, 2s."

The town of Market Harborough, Leicestershire, sent its soldiers to the muster in Leicester in 1613.[18] Some of the expenses that it incurred included 4d for 1 oz of "cruel" to make the fringes of the pikes, 3d for having the fringes made, and 10d for a piece of red cloth for the town's pikes.

12   Leicester Record Office, Records of the Borough of Leicester, BR/II/18/12, f.16.
13   Corporation of Nottingham, *Records of the Borough of Nottingham*, Vol. 4 (London: Bernard Quaritch, 1884), p.346.
14   Corporation of Nottingham, *Records of the Borough of Nottingham*, Vol. 4, p.352.
15   Nottingham, Corporation of, *Records of the Borough of Nottingham*, Vol. 5 (London: Bernard Quaritch, 1900), p.120.
16   British Library, Add MS 6702, f.116.
17   Kent History and Library Centre, Gr/Fac/1, folios 101, 108, 110.
18   J.E. Stocks, *Market Harborough Parish Records 1531–1837* (London:Oxford University Press, 1926), pp.64, 129–130.

For the muster in 1614, the town of Leicester paid 2s 6d for cotton to arm some of the town's pikes and another 2s 6d was paid for blue cloth to arm some of the pikes.[19] Whether this was a double entry is not made clear but what is clear is that blue cloth was used by the town of Leicester for its pikes.

The musters in Leicester in 1615 entailed more expenditure by the town[20]. Leicester paid for 44 yards of white ribbon and another 44 yards of "watched" ribbon. The white ribbon cost 6d per yard, the cost of the other ribbon is not known but the overall cost was £2. This was given to the town's 40 soldiers as favours to distinguish them from the rest of the Trained Band, it was noted that every captain had his own colour.

A letter was sent from Sir Edmond Mundford to Sir William de Grey, a deputy lieutenant and commander of the foot company in Wayland Hundred, Norfolk in June 1621.[21] Sir Edmond informed Sir William that he was sending his two pikemen to the company muster, but noted "I know not with what colour you will have your pikes armed and therefore have left them bare until I hear from you."

A short document held in the Somerset Heritage Centre for the "Arming for pikes" for the soldiers in Hemiock Parish in Devon says that the colours to be used were blue and yellow,[22] and these colours were to be provided by the owners of the pikes. The document is undated but is from the first half of the seventeenth century.

The Deepwade Hundred Company in Norfolk was commanded by Sir Thomas Knyvett from 1601 until his death in 1605; from then until at least 1621 Sir Ralph Shelton was in command,[23] from 1626 until at least 1640 Thomas Knyvett, Esq. (1596–1658) of Ashwellthorpe was the captain, in the Civil War he was a Royalist sympathiser. The hundred is located to the south of Norwich, midway between the city and the Suffolk border. In 1605 the company numbered 200 soldiers and 20 pioneers, and in 1626 still numbered 200 men comprised of 80 pikemen, 120 musketeers with 22 pioneers. These numbers were the same in 1627 and 1628. Sir Thomas mentioned the captain's colours in a letter to his wife in May/June 1627.[24] In the letter he described a hat he was buying for her, "a delicate hatt & white fether for so it must be, only it shall have a little tippe of yr captaines colours". He does not say what the colours were, but from the wording it would seem that there were at least two.

In Rev. Godwin's *The Civil War in Hampshire*[25] there is a reference to the costs of equipping soldiers, foot and horse, dating to 1628. They refer to the cost of a pike being the staff 2s 6d and then the cost of the head, socket and colouring.

---

19 Leicester Record Office, Records of the Borough of Leicester, BR/III/2/76.
20 Leicester Record Office, Records of the Borough of Leicester, BR/II/18/12, f.2.
21 Norfolk Record Office, WLS XVII/2,410X5.
22 Somerset Heritage Centre, DD WO 56/6/45-5.
23 British Library, King's MS 265.
24 Bertram Schofield (ed.), *The Knyvett Letters, 1620–1644* (Bishop's Stortford: Norfolk Record Society, 1949), Volume XX, pp.72–73.
25 Rev G.N. Godwin, *The Civil War in Hampshire (1642–45) and the Story of Basing House* (Southampton: 1904, revised edition).

At some point during 1633 or 1634, Nottingham's trained band was mustered and trained. The captain and lieutenant of the company these men belonged to were paid 12s for the time they spent with the men. The town also paid 14s 6d for colours for the men when they trained, what these colours were for is not made clear.[26] In previous years Nottingham had paid out for ribbons for its soldiers.

A number of references exist regarding pike colouring in the Leicestershire Trained Band; the earliest is from Wymeswold in 1627.[27] Wymeswold had seven soldiers, three of whom were pikemen and four were musketeers. Among the costs for the musters in 1627 is an entry that says 4s was paid for the soldiers' colours, and the same amount was noted in 1628. The final entry concerning the soldiers' colours was noted in 1640. The entry reads, "Paid for the soldiers' colours, 7 men, 8s 2d".

The village of Branston, in north-east Leicestershire, in 1639 recorded paying 6d to have its pike coloured. The village only provided one soldier to the trained band.[28] Lastly, in March 1639 in the village of Stathern, also in north-east Leicestershire, 1s was spent in colouring the village's two pikes. This work was done in nearby Melton Mowbray. At the same time the village spent 1s 6d having sockets fitted to its headpieces, although whether this was for all four of their soldiers or just two of them is not recorded.[29] A socket would indicate the intended use of a feather, coloured perhaps, or some such similar item.

The 5th Marquess of Winchester, John Paulet, had an armoury at Basing House, and an inventory taken on 14 January 1639 listed a considerable amount of arms and armour there.[30] Among the less modern arms listed were 11 white bills, armed, six with the falcon, a symbol of the Paulet family. How the image of the falcon was applied to the bills is not known.

Standards/Colours

In 1619 the Bristol Corporation bought new armour and equipment for 30 men in the trained band. The cost of this was 22s 6d per corslet and 12 to 15s per musket. They also bought one new colour at a cost of £8 5s, a drum for £2 12s and half a ton of gunpowder at 9½d per pound.[31]

In August 1627 there was a proposal that the City of London should raise four regiments of archers as per people's obligations under the Statute 33rd Henry VIII, which made archery practice compulsory.[32] Each captain was to have an "Ancient of taffatie in colour"

26 Corporation of Nottingham, *Records of the Borough of Nottingham*, Vol. 5, p.164.
27 British Library, Add MS 10457, ff.37, 84.
28 Leicester Record Office, Branston Constables Accounts – DE720-30, f.44.
29 Leicester Record Office, Stathern Constables Accounts DE1605/56.
30 British Library, Add MS 69907C, f.39.
31 John Latimer, *The Annals of Bristol in the seventeenth century* (Bristol: William George's Sons, 1887), pp.70–71.
32 H.C. Overall and W.H. Overall, *Analytical index to the series of records known as the Remembrancia*, pp.17–18.

The Bristol Corporation bought two new colours for two of its captains in 1633 or 1634, these cost almost £30 for the two. The two recipients were Captain Richard Aldworth and Captain Giles Elbridge.[33]

On 9 June 1639, Manchester paid for repair of the town's trained band company's colours with calico and silk, this cost 6s.[34]

In *The Souldiers Exercise: in three bookes*, written by Gervase Markham and published in 1639, there is some guidance on colours that can be used.[35] Markham does say that two colours are all that is needed.

To date the present author has not found any definitive descriptions of pre-Civil War colours. However, author Stephen Ede-Borrett, who has undertaken extensive research on the flags of this period, believes that amongst the colours shown in British Library Sloane MS 5247 are a number of pre-Civil War trained band colours.[36]

33 Latimer, *The Annals of Bristol in the seventeenth century*, p.115.
34 J.P. Earwaker, *The Constables' Accounts of the Manor of Manchester from the year 1612 to the year 1647*, Vol. 1 (Manchester: Cornish, 1892), p.65.
35 Gervase Markham, *The Souldiers Exercise in three books* (London: 1643; reprinted by Partizan Press, 2013), pp.29–34.
36 Personal communication between the author and Stephen Ede-Borrett.

Rame home

16

Put your scouring stick downe
into your Musket and Ramme
home hard twice or thrice

8

Arms, Armour and Equipment

During the early seventeenth century, warfare changed as lessons were learned from the fighting on the Continent: the Eighty Years' War had started in 1568 and the Thirty Years' War in 1618, and both were to continue until 1648. Many men from the British Isles went abroad to fight in these wars for one side or the other and some of these men returned home to pass on what they had learned. One lesson passed on was that the weapons of the trained bands had to be up to date, and for the foot this meant muskets of a standard bore, and pikes of the correct length. Calivers were effectively banned from the trained bands from 1619 but were still noted in some of the poorer counties and being provided by the clergy and also in the untrained bands. The horse also needed to be modernised but this was a problem that seemed to have no workable solution. Attempts to standardise the trained band arms and armour occurred a number of times. In 1626 a Parliamentary order detailed the specifications for the arms and armour to be used by the trained bands; the details of this are included in the various following sections.[1] An instruction issued by the Council of War in 1635 was another attempt at standardisation and modernisation, again the details for the various arms and armour are included here.[2]

In 1603 the main types of arms used by the trained band foot were pikes (carried by men either armoured or unarmoured) and shot (muskets and calivers). There were other, older, weapons still in use but in small numbers and these were being phased out of service with the selected soldiers of the trained bands. Many of these older weapons were still being used by the untrained men associated with the trained bands and their use was occasionally enforced.

While some of the basic equipment for the trained soldiers did not change very much over the 40 years before the Civil War, some of the costs did. There are a number of lists showing the equipment for the foot soldiers and their associated costs. Of the four used here the first list comes from Yorkshire and

---

1   Rye, *State papers relating to musters*, pp.89–91.
2   Rye, *State papers relating to musters*, pp.199–203.

is dated 1605,[3] one comes from Brecon, probably in 1608,[4] one from Suffolk in 1632/3[5] but originally published in 1628,[6] and the last from the Earl of Huntingdon's armoury in 1633.[7] Of particular note is the description of testing a corslet and a pike in the Suffolk section.

The Foot

Archery, Longbow

Officially the longbow was withdrawn from service in the trained bands in 1595, although it had been in decline for some time before then. Despite this it did continue to appear in some muster rolls in the early part of the seventeenth century.

In 1606 the muster roll for Ryedale Wapentake in the North Riding of Yorkshire included nine archers, all private soldiers, not common soldiers.[8] In the same year the men in Gotham, Nottinghamshire, were fined 1s each because the village did not have any butts for practising their archery.[9] One of the companies in the Kingsclere Regiment in Hampshire fielded archers equipped with longbows and billmen in 1612, and again in 1616, but these were part of the untrained element of the company.[10] From the way the muster book is written it is possible that these men were not part of the selected band but unselected men although still part of the company. It should also be pointed out that there is a note in the 1616 muster book to the effect that none of the archers attended the muster. They claimed that they had been told that archers were no longer required and that they only had to have their other equipment on hand with their main weapon now being a sword. The untrained band in Cheshire in 1613 still contained archers. Of the 500 men in the untrained band, 44 were armed with bows.[11]

In October 1621 a number of the male inhabitants of Husbands Bosworth in Leicestershire were fined 6s 8d each for failing to practise with the longbow.[12] The constable was also fined 6d for not enforcing the statute requiring them to shoot. It should be noted here that the Privy Council did call for 480 men armed with longbows to be raised for the Isle of Rhé expedition in 1627;[13] that year there was a proposal in London that four regiments of archers should be raised there, though there is no evidence to suggest that this happened.[14] Despite the drive to update the arms of the trained bands, Charles did issue a

---

3   British Library, Add MS 36293, ff.93–94.
4   British Library, Add MS 10609.
5   Bodleian Library, Tanner MS 71/f.131.
6   Huntington Library, Bridgwater Collection, MSS EL7617.
7   Huntington Library, Hastings Collection, HA inventories Box 1(7) & (9).
8   British Library, Add MS 36293, ff.103–5.
9   Copnall and Saxton, *Nottinghamshire County Records*, p.91.
10   Hampshire Record Office, 44M69/G5/20/102/1 & 44M69/G5/21/1.
11   The National Archives, SP 16/117, f.32.
12   Leicestershire Records Office, DG39/678.
13   Lyle, *Acts of the Privy Council of England, 1627, January–August*, pp.500–1.
14   H.C. Overall and W.H. Overall, *Analytical index to the series of records known as the Remembrancia*, p.19.

commission reactivating the requirement for all able-bodied men to practice with the longbow in 1628,[15] only to revoke this in 1631.[16] This may have been a pretext to raise money, however, as failure to practise archery was still an offence for which men could be fined as at Husbands Bosworth. In 1640 archers were still being requested by Charles from Leicestershire and other counties after the rout in the north, although whether they were available is another matter. In April 1641 Maurice Wynn in Carnarvonshire wrote to his brother Owen at Gwydir, Carnarvonshire, concerning arms and armour that he had sent to Chester. The list included powder, muskets, pikes, headpieces, swords and bows and arrows.[17]

Double-Armed Man or Bow-Pike

Another proclamation issued in 1633[18] supported the use of the bow-pike by the county trained bands, something which Nottinghamshire was still discussing in 1638. The bow-pike was an attempt to give the pike an offensive capability, referred to as the "double-armed man".[19] Basically a longbow was attached to the pike shaft by a swivel. The man responsible for this was William Neade and he published a book promoting his invention in 1625. This allowed the pikeman to rest the base of the pike against his right foot, he held the pike and bow in his left hand and drew the bow with his right hand. A fairly large number of members of the Westminster and London artillery gardens were trained in the use of this and in 1633 they gave a demonstration to the King. Charles apparently joined in and was sufficiently impressed to issue the proclamation calling for the weapon to be adopted by the trained bands.

Calivers

The following description of a caliver comes from Yorkshire, dated to 1602, but being used in 1605:

> A caliver of double proof, smooth bored and in good extraordinary with trigger, lock, mould, worm and screw, the stock walnut tree, a bullet bag, a bandoleer of double plait. A sword, right Turkey with good basket hilt burnished within & without with a fishskin handle and a double scabbard and chape and a girdle and hangers. Finally, a morion of the best English, well lined & stringed.[20]

The 1626 Parliamentary order detailed the specifications for the calivers despite them not being used by the trained bands by this time. They were to have a barrel with a length of not less than 3½ feet, the bore of the barrel was to be able to take a ball with the weight of 17 to the pound. The rest of

---

15 27 Mar 1628, Calendar of State Papers, Domestic Series, Vol. XCVIII, p.43.
16 23 Aug 1631, Woodstock, Calendar of State Papers, Domestic Series, Vol. CXCVIII, p.134.
17 Calendar of Wynn (of Gwydir) papers, 1515–1690 in the National Library of Wales and elsewhere, Aberyswyth, Cardiff and London, 1926, f.1683.
18 William Salt Library, A proclamation for the use of the bow and pike together, S.1557/243, dated 12 August 1633.
19 See E.T. Fox, *Military Archery in the Seventeenth Century: Three Seventeenth-century Texts* (n.p.: Lulu.com, 2015).
20 British Library, Add MS 36293, f.100.

the caliver equipment was to include a bandoleer with 15 charges of turned wood covered with leather with a good fastener. Other equipment was to be a bullet bag, a primer, worm, scourer and a mould to cast the correctly sized musket balls or bullets. His sword was to have a blade not more than three feet in length and to be sharp. The only armour to be worn was to be a morion or other headpiece.

The 1635 order included instructions for the caliver despite it having been barred from use in the trained bands in 1619. The specifications for it were the same as in 1626.

Bastard Musket

The bastard musket falls somewhere between the caliver and the musket. Unlike the musket, it did not need a rest.

This description of a bastard musket, dated to 1602, comes from Yorkshire:

> A bastard musket of double proof, smooth bored and in goodness extraordinary with trigger, lock, mould, screw and worm, the stock walnut tree, a bullet bag, a bandoleer of double plait in goodness extraordinary with large and strong girdles and strings. A sword, right Turkey with good basket hilt burnished within & without with a fishskin handle and a double scabbard and chape and a girdle and hangers. Finally, a morion of the best English, well lined & stringed.[21]

In the Cinque Ports bastard muskets were phased out by 1632 and swords and daggers by 1629.[22]

Musketeers

This description of a musketeer's arms and armour comes from Yorkshire and Brecon and is a combination of two documents dated to 1602[23] and about 1608[24] respectively. They are so close that they have been put together here. The description is as follows:

> A musket of double proof, smooth bored with trigger, lock, mould and worm, the stock walnut tree and in goodness extraordinary, a rest, a bullet bag, a bandoleer of double plait in goodness extraordinary with large and strong girdles and strings. A sword, right Turkey with good basket hilt burnished within & without with a fishskin handle and a double scabbard and chape and a girdle and hangers.

Finally, "a morion of the best English, well lined & stringed".

The 1626 Parliamentary order detailed the specifications for the arms and armour to be used by the trained bands musketeers were as follows. The muskets were to have a barrel with a length of exactly four feet, the bore was to be able to take a ball with the weight of 11 to the pound. The rest of the musketeer's equipment was to include a bandoleer with 15 charges of turned

---

21 British Library, Add MS 36293, f.100.
22 East Sussex Record Office, RYE85/15–18.
23 British Library, Add MS 36293, f.100.
24 British Library, BL Add 10609.

wood covered with leather with a good fastener. Other equipment was to be a bullet bag, a primer, worm, scourer and a mould to cast the correctly sized musket balls or bullets. The musket rest was to be 4½ feet in length. His sword was to have a blade not more than three feet in length and be sharp. The only armour to be worn was a morion or other headpiece.

A muster roll from Devon for 1632 lists the men and the arms and armour provided for them, for the South Molton Hundred.[25] The people who provided the arms and armour are also listed, which tells us how the men were equipped and by how many people. The musketeer's equipment included the musket, rest, bandoleers, sword, girdle, hangers, belt, bag, mould and headpiece referred to as a morion in a number of cases.

The 1635 order for the musketeers included some changes from those issued in 1626 as well as a few extra details. The muskets were to have a total length of five feet two inches with the barrel still four feet long but now the bore was 12 bullets to the pound, rolling in, indicating a slightly smaller bore.

Pikemen

Pikemen came in two varieties, armoured and unarmoured. The armoured pikemen were usually referred to simply as corslets which was the armour that they wore. The unarmoured pikemen were often referred to as dry pikes, which as far as can be ascertained, reflects the Spanish term *pica seca*. This term had been in use since at least the start of the Eighty Years' War in the Netherlands.

Descriptions of the arms used by the armoured and unarmoured pikemen and the armour worn by the armoured pikemen, while not common, are available. Some of these are what was actually used and others are what was officially required.

The first two descriptions are almost the same, the first comes from Yorkshire and is dated 1602,[26] the other one comes from Brecon, probably in 1608.[27] In the description of the pikeman for these two counties, the arms and the armour were described as:

> The back, breast, collar and headpiece, all of English making and of the best for metal & exposition, especially good pauldrons and a pair of tassets, with the best English pikestaff with the head well steeled and long bladed, a sword right Turkey with good basket hilt burnished within & without with a fishskin handle and a double scabbard and chape, a girdle and hangers of black, grained leather especially good and large.

The 1626 Parliamentary order required the pike to be made of ash, 18 feet long and have a diameter, at the middle, of at least 1¾ inches. The head of the pike was to be steel, eight inches in length, it was to be broad and sword pointed with the cheeks being at least two feet in length. The butt of the pike was to have an iron ring on it. Ideally the pikeman should be armoured,

25   Devon Heritage Centre, Z19/46/7.
26   British Library, Add MS 36293, f.100.
27   British Library, BL Add 10609.

the main item being a corslet and the 1626 order described this. The corslet should consist of a good breast plate and a back piece and an iron gorget. The tassets should be deep-skirted and not more than nine inches in length and 13 inches in width. They should be attached to the skirt of the breast plate with good strong buckles. Pouldrons were out of fashion by 1626, so these were not required. The last item of armour was a good morion or headpiece. The pikeman's other equipment included a good sword, no more than three feet in length in a good scabbard fitted to a belt or girdle with hangers.

The muster roll from Devon for 1632 for the Hundred of South Molton gives us the following information on their pikeman.[28] His equipment included the pike, corslet, sword and belt; the corslet included the morion headpiece – although a burgonet was used by one man – gorget, cuirasses and the tasses.

The 1635 order for the pikeman only changed a little from 1626. The dimensions of the pike remained the same, except that the overall length of the pike was now to be 17 feet.

Targets, Sword and Buckler

Men armed with a target (a small shield), were regularly seen during the Italian Wars in the sixteenth century. By the start of the seventeenth century they were very much in decline but still appearing in the ranks of some of the trained bands until at least 1622. The men provided by the clergy in the county of Brecon in 1617 were organised as a small county-wide company, and the 100 men who formed this company included four targeteers.[29] In Anglesey, also in 1617, a muster of the trained and untrained men was held. Of the 699 men present, 33 were reported as being armed as targeteers.[30] In the town of Shrewsbury in Shropshire, two of the soldiers were attending the musters armed as targeteers until at least 1622.

Bills

Bills were not used by the trained bands in the seventeenth century or at least not by the selected soldiers, but by the pioneers and the untrained soldiers. The general musters for the Cinque Ports show a wide variety of obsolete arms and armour being brought to the musters, besides the expected muskets and corslets, although they were being carried by the untrained men. Until at least 1634 the untrained men in the Cinque Ports were still being charged with bills and sculls or headpieces as well as dry pikes, pairs of curats and halberds.[31]

The bills were variously described as brown bills, black bills, Welsh bills or simply as bills. The differences were not explained and no description was given for any of these.

---

28 Devon Heritage Centre, Z19/46/7.
29 British Library, Add MS 10609, ff.45–46.
30 National Library of Wales, Carreglwyd Estate Records, Tallabollion Hundred, 25th September 1616.
31 East Sussex Record Office, RYE85/15–18.

The Horse

From 1603 the types of horsemen found in the trained bands were variously named as carbine, cuirassier, lancer, light horseman, petronel, harquebusier and dragoon. Many counties raised more than one type of horseman, and the equipment for these men is shown below.

Carbine

The 1635 order included specifications for a carbine. His main weapon was a harquebus or a petronel, this was to have an overall length of 3¾ feet, with the barrel being 2½ feet long and firing a bullet at 17 to the pound, rolling in. There was no armour except that he had to have a buff coat and a belt with an iron swivel to hang his harquebus or petronel from. He was also to have a sword. His horse was to be a medium sized gelding or a nag. The mention of a petronel is interesting as by this date they were obsolete.

Cuirassier

The cuirassiers were also sometimes as referred to as pistoleers. The 1626 Parliamentary order required the armour of a cuirassier to be comprised of a good cask and gorget, an iron breast plate and back piece, pistol proof, these should have strong buckles to fasten on the pouldrons, tassets, cuishes (thigh guard), a cullet (rear lower back guard) and vambraces, all made of iron. He should also have a left-hand gauntlet and be armed with a case of firelock pistols with a barrel of at least two feet three inches in length. The bore of the pistol was to be 36 bullets to the pound and no more, he was also to have a flask and touchbox. His other weapon was a sharp sword of at least four feet in length. The horse or gelding had to be strong and large enough to carry the cuirassier, and to have a strong saddle.

The next list of arms and armour for a cuirassier comes from Suffolk in a document dated 1632/3,[32] but originally published in 1628 as the result of an instruction from the Council of War,[33] The cuirassier's armour was to comprise a back and breast plate, both pistol proof, a lined gorget, a close cask, lined, a pair of pouldrons, vambraces and cuisetts, a cullet or guarderers and a gloved gauntlet. He was also to have a pair of firelock pistols, furnished with a key, mould, scourer, worm, flask and cases of leather, the barrel was to be of a foot and a half long. The stock and all were to measure about 26 inches, the bullet to weigh 24 to the pound, rolling in.

The 1635 order for the cuirassier's armour did not differ significantly from the 1626 order, except that a buff jerkin with long skirts was now required to be worn under the armour. The man's arms however, had not changed except for his sword which was now to be 3½ feet in length.

---

32 Bodleian Library, Tanner MS 71/folio 131.
33 Huntington Library, Bridgwater Collection, MSS EL7617.

Harquebusier

The 1626 Parliamentary order called for the harquebusier to be armed with a petronel or harquebus, with a firelock, and a barrel at least three feet long. The bore was to be 20 bullets to the pound. He was also to have a good flask and touchbox and a strong belt to hang his petronel or harquebus from. Other arms included a pair of pistols of the same type as the cuirassier. His armour was to be a good head piece, a gorget and a back piece and a breast plate that was pistol proof. The horse or gelding had to be strong, large and have a strong saddle.

The next list of arms and armour for a harquebusier comes from Suffolk in a document dated 1632/3[34] but originally published in 1628 as the result of an instruction from the Council of War.[35] The harquebusier's armour was to be russeted and to consist of a breast plate that was pistol proof, a back plate, a gorget and a head piece with large cheek pieces and a single bar for face protection. At this time the harquebusier could be armed with a carbine or a harquebus both fitted with a firelock. The barrel was to be at least 2½ feet long but preferably three feet long with a 15 inch stock. The bore was to be 17 bullets to the pound with a powder charge of no more than two thirds of the bullet weight. The tools for the weapon were to include a belt with a swivel, a flask, a key, a bullet mould, a worm & a scourer. In addition he was to have a pair of horseman's pistols furnished with a snaphance, a mould, a worm, a scourer, a flask, a charger and cases.

The 1635 order for the harquebusier showed a number of changes to his arms and armour. His main weapon, the harquebus, was now to have an overall length of 3¾ feet, with the barrel being 2½ feet long and firing a slightly heavier bullet at 17 to the pound. His armour no longer included a gorget but he now had to have a buff jerkin to wear underneath his back and breast plate, still pistol proof.

Lancer

The first two descriptions for a lancer come from Yorkshire, dated 1602,[36] and from Brecon, probably from 1608.[37] The rider's armour was to be comprised of "a close caske of the best English, cuishes, pauldrons and vambraces and two great gauntlets". His arms were to include "a French pistol of double proof, smooth bored with mould, worm and screw with a case of the best leather and a flask of horn with double head as well as a sword right Turkey with a girdle and hangers and a lance staff with the head well steeled".

Light Horseman

The first two descriptions for a light horseman come from Yorkshire, dated 1602,[38] and from Brecon, probably from 1608.[39] The rider's armour was to comprise a "cuvett with back, breast, collar and burgonet in goodness

---

34　Bodleian Library, Tanner MS 71/f.131.
35　Huntington Library, Bridgwater Collection, MSS EL7617.
36　British Library, Add MS 36293, f.100.
37　British Library, BL Add 10609.
38　British Library, Add MS 36293, f.100.
39　British Library, BL Add 10609.

extraordinary, pouldrons extraordinary and an especially good elbow gauntlet". His arms were to be:

[a] pistol double proof, smooth bored with mould, worm and screw in a case of the best and strongest good leather with a monkey head top with a flask of horn with double head, a sword right Turkey with an extraordinary arming hilt the best fish skinned handle with double scabbard and chape and a girdle and hangers of black grained leather and a staff with head well steeled.

This would indicate that in the first decade of the seventeenth century, the light horseman was armed as a lancer.

The next description for a light horseman's equipment comes from Hertford in 1611.[40] The rider was to be equipped with a pair of curats, a gorget, a burgonet, a light horseman's staff, a sword, a dagger and a case of pistols or at least one pistol.

Petronel

The petronel was named after his main weapon, the petronel, a long-barreled firearm intended to be fired from the chest rather than the shoulder. It was a sixteenth-century weapon and this type of horseman had disappeared by 1627, being converted to light horsemen in most cases.

Dragoon

The term dragoon seems to have been used interchangeably with harquebusier throughout this period, although the two types were supposed to have had a different battlefield role. A list of the arms for a dragoon used in Denbigh in 1629 says that they should have:

[a] good harquebus or a dragoone fitted with an iron work to be carried in a belt with a flask, priming box, key and bullet bag, an open head to mount on a piece with cheeks, a good buff coat with deep skirts, sword, girdle and hangers, a saddle, bridle, bit, petrel, crupper with straps for his sack of necessaries and a good horse.[41]

Interestingly, from the same source but two years later, in 1631, the "arms of a harquebusier or dragoon" are listed. The fact that the two appear to be interchangeable is of note. The list is as follows:

The arms of a harquebusier or dragoon which hath succeeded in the place of light horsemen (and are indeed of singular use almost in all actions of war) the arms are a good harquebus or a dragoone fitted with an iron work to be carried in a belt, a belt with a flask, priming box, key and bullet bag, an open head to mount on a piece with cheeks, a good buff coat with deep skirts, sword, girdle and hangers, a saddle, bridle, bit, petrel, crupper with straps for his sack of necessaries and a horse of less force and less price than the cuirassier.

---

40 Green, *Calendar of State Papers, Domestic Series, 1611–1618*, p.73.
41 National Library of Wales, Chirk B, 91a musters, 1629–35.

The Costs

Of the four lists used here the first list comes from Yorkshire and is dated 1602,[42] one comes from Brecon, probably in 1608,[43] one from Suffolk in 1632/3[44] but originally published in 1628,[45] and the last from the Earl of Huntingdon's armoury in 1633.[46] Of particular note is the description of testing a corslet and a pike in the Suffolk section.

Table 27. The pikeman's arms and armour

Equipment	1602/8*
Corslet	15s
Pouldrons	4s 4d
Pike	3s 4d
Sword right Turkey with good basket hilt burnished within & without with a fishskin handle and a double scabbard and chape	9s 6d
A pair of tassets	2s
A girdle and hangers	1s 10d
Total	£1 16s

* British Library, Add MS 36293, f.100, and Add MS 10609

The musketeers in Yorkshire and Brecon, from 1605 to about 1608, were equipped with the following:

Table 28. Musketeers' equipment, Yorkshire and Brecon

Equipment	1602/8
A musket of double proof, smooth bored with trigger, lock, mould and worm, the stock walnut tree and in goodness extraordinary	17s
A rest	8d
A bullet bag	4d
A morion of the best English, well lined & stringed	3s 4d
Bandoleer of double plait in goodness extraordinary with large and strong girdles and strings.	2s
A sword right Turkey in due condition as the pikeman's	9s 6d
Girdle and hangers as the pikeman's	1s 10d
Sum total of the musket complete	£1 14s 8d

42   British Library, Add MS 36293, f.100.
43   British Library, BL Add 10609.
44   Bodleian Library, Tanner MS 71/f.131.
45   Huntington Library, Bridgwater Collection, MSS EL7617.
46   Huntington Library, Hastings Collection, HA inventories Box 1(7) & (9).

Table 29. Equipment for a "bastard musket"

Equipment	1602
Bastard musket of double proof, smooth bored and in goodness extraordinary with trigger, lock, mould worm and screw and the stock walnut.	16s 8d
Bullet bag	4d
A morion of the best English, well lined & stringed	3s 4d
Bandoleer of double plaite *ut anter*	1s 10d
A sword right Turkey *ut anter*	9s 6d
Girdle and hangers *ut anter*	1s 10d
Total	£1 13s 6d

Table 30. Equipment for a caliver

Equipment	1602/8
A caliver of double proof, smooth bored in goodness extraordinary with trigger, lock, mould, worm and screw, the stock walnut tree	12s 2d
A bullet bag	4d
A morion of the best English, well lined and stringed.	3s 4d
Bandoleer of double plait	1s 10d
A sword right Turkey *ut anter*	9s 6d
Girdle and hangers *ut anter*	1s 10d
Sum total of the caliver complete	£1 9s

Table 31. Equipment for a light horseman

Equipment	1602/8
Cuvett with back, breast, collar and burgonet in goodness extraordinary	£1
Pouldrons extraordinary	5s 6d
An especially good elbow gauntlet	6s 6d
Pistol double proof, smooth bored with mould, worm and screw.	17s 6d
Case of the best and strongest good leather with a monke(y) head top	3s 2d
Flask of horn with double head	3s
A staff with head well steeled	3s
A sword right Turkey with an extraordinary arming hilt the best fish skinned handle with double scabbard and chape	9s 6d
A girdle and hangers of black grained leather *ut antra*	1s 10d
Sum total of the light horse complete	£3 11s

Table 32. Equipment for a lancer

Equipment	1602/8
A close caske of the best English	17s
Cushes	12s
2 great gauntlets	8s
Pouldrons and Vambraces	12s
Lance staff with the head well steeled	5s
A French pistol of double proof, smooth bored with mould, worm and screw.	17s 6d
Case of the best leather *ut anter*	3s 2d
Flask of horn with double head	3s
A sword right Turkey *ut anter*	9s 6d
A girdle and hangers *ut antra*	1s 10d
Sum total of lance armour complete	£5

The 1628 list from Suffolk has a number of interesting points, namely two sets of prices indicating that some negotiation went on between the sellers and buyers and the methods of testing the pike and the breast plate. Specifications for various weapons are also included, see Table 33.

Proof of the Staff
"If the pique be taken with the left hand close to the head, the right hand not above one foot removed from the left & 5 or 6 times shaken with the full strength of an able man, it is held allowable proof of the staff."

Proof of the Head
"For proof of the head, it is conceived that if the pique be advanced with the point downwards & diverse times perpendicularly, let fall upon an iron or steel plate placed 3 foot under, it will appear whether the head be well steeled or not."

"The length, 4 feet. The length of a butt and of a musquett stock from the [barrel] backwards to be 14 inches," see also Table 34.

Charge of the Bandoleer

For diverse weapons & from good experience it is conceived the content of each charger of the bandoleer for field service be reduced to half the weight of the rolling bullet where 12 do make the pound.

To discharge with any assurance from a parapitt

⅔ or ¾ of the bullet' weight at the most, is conceived a sufficient quantity of powder for a musquetier to discharge any assurance from a parapitt.

Table 33. Specifications for weapons, 1628

The prices of the severall parts & whole armor for a cuirassier russeted established by a committee of the Councell of warre anno 1628	The prices demanded by the Artificers			The prices reduced by the Councell of Warre		
	£	s	d	£	s	d
A back of pistol prooffe	00	09	00	00	07	00
A breast of pistol prooffe	00	13	00	00	11	00
A close casque lined	00	18	00	00	17	00
A paire of pouldrons	00	13	00	00	12	00
A pair of vambraces	00	13	00	00	12	00
A paire of cuisetts	00	18	00	00	17	00
A culet or guarderers	00	08	00	00	07	00
A gorget lined	00	04	00	00	03	06
A gauntlet gloved	00	04	00	00	03	06
	05	00	00	04	10	00

Low country price from £5 to £7. So the whole price of a cuirassier's armour to be delivered at London will amount unto: £4 10s 0d
The price of a pair of firelock pistols, furnished with a key, mould, scourer, worm, flask & cases of leather, the barrel to be of a foot & a half long: Stock & all about 26 inches, the bullet of 24 in the pound, rolling in. Demanded £ 5s 0d. Reduced to £3 0s 0d

The prices of the parts & of the whole armour for an Harquebusier on horseback russetted.	The prices demanded by the Artificers			The prices reduced by the Councell of Warre					
A breast of pistol prooffe	00	13	00	00	11	00			
A back	00	08	00	00	07	00			
A gorgett	00	04	00	00	03	06			
A headpiece with great cheeks & a barre before his face	00	12	00	00	11	00			
	01	17	00	01	12	06			

The total of all the parts & of the whole Armour for a harquebusier is £1 12s 6d.
The Low Country price from 50s to £3.
The price of a Harquebuze or Carabyne with a firelock & belt, swivel flasque, key, mould, worme & scowrer, £2 0s 0d / £1 16s 0d
For a paire of horsemans pistols furnished with a snaphance, mould, worme, scowrer, flasque, charger & cases. £2 2s 0d / £2 0s 0d
The barrel 2½ feet long or rather 3 feet long, the stocke from the breech backwards, 15 inches.
The bore of 17 in the pound rolling in.
The lading of powder not above ⅔ of the bullets weight.
The price of a carbine with a snaphance, belt, swivel, flask, key, mould, worm & scourer; Demanded £1 2s 0d, reduced £1 1s 0d

The prices of the parts & of the whole corslet or footman's armour rateable.	Prices demanded			Prices reduced		
The breast	00	06	00	00	05	06
The back	00	05	00	00	04	06

		00	05	00	00	05	00
The tassets		00	05	00	00	05	00
The combed headpiece, lined		00	05	00	00	04	06
The gorget, lined		00	03	00	00	02	06
		01	04	00	01	02	00

The total price of a footman's armour, £1 2s 0d
The Low Country price, 24s to 25s.
If the breast, back and tassets be lined with red leather the price will be; £1 4s 0d
Paid by the King for back, breast, gorget & headpiece; £0 19s 0d
The English price of tassets; £0 5s 0d
Which together made; £1 4s 0d
Proof of the corslet
It is conceived that if a pike be advanced with the point downwards & diverse times perpendicularly let fall upon a corslet, placed 3 foot or more under, it will appear whether the corslet be good or not.
The Pique (pike)
The staff is to be 16 foot long.
The diameter of the staff at the ordering place betwixt 5 & 6 foot from the butt end, no less than one inch & a half.
The head to be 8 inches in length, broad, strong, sword pointed & well steeled.
The cheeks to be 2 foot in length well riveted.
The butt end bound with a taper socket of iron for the better planting of the pique.

The price of the pike vizt	
The staff	2s 6d
The head	1s 8d
The socket & colouring	0s 4d

Table 34. Costs of a musket

Musquett	Prices demanded	Prices reduced
For a new musquett with mold, worme & scowrer	£0 16s 0d	£0 15s 6d

Proof of the Musquett

"So much powder as shall equal the weight of the bullet whereof ten do make the pound, the bullet with an iron rammer being driven close to the powder. It is conceived to be a very warrantable proofe for the musquet, especially if twice proved with good powder before it bee allowed."

Bandoliers

"For a new bandolier with 12 charges, a primer & a priming wire, a bullet bagge & a strappe or belt & 2 inches in breadth; 2s 6d" (the breakdown of the charges is shown Table 35).

Table 35. Cost of bandoliers

The particulars thus;	s	d
The strappe	1	0
The Bagge	0	1
Strings & priming iron	0	3
For 12 charges	1	2
Total	2	6

Following the 1623 musters in Hampshire, it was reported that the county required new arms and armour for both the horse and foot.[47] The costs for the new equipment and the costs for repairs for some of the existing equipment were provided, possibly as a guide. These were as follows, see Table 36:

Table 36. Cost for new equipment and repairs, Hampshire 1623

	s	d
Gorget, curat, tasses and headpiece	31	0
A pike made of ash	6	6
Musket	18	0
Bandoleer	2	0
Sword	6	0
Belt	2	0
Headpiece	3	4
Rest	1	0
Stocking of a piece	2	6
Mending the lock	2	6
Tasses	8	0

For the Leicestershire county muster in 1615, Thomas Wynbie was paid £1 14s 11d for "fringing" the men's headpieces and lining them with broad cloth.[48] This seems to indicate that steel caps were bought and altered locally.

Notes

The terminology used regarding the weapons should be noted. The pike and the pikeman's equipment seem to have attracted the larger number of terms. These are as follows:

Armed pike, this describes a pike that has been probably painted with the colours of the captain whose company uses it.

Bare pike, an uncommon term probably used to describe an unarmoured pikeman, similar to the dry pike.

Corslet, a term used to describe a pikeman with full armour protection. The word corslet was from a French word for body armour from the sixteenth century.

Dry pike, this referred to a pikeman who was unarmoured or lightly armoured. This description was being used by the Spanish Army during

---

47 Hampshire Record Office, 4M53/140, f.137.
48 Leicester Record Office, Records of the Borough of Leicester, BR/III/2/77, f.33.

the Italian Wars in the sixteenth century, the Spanish term being *pica seca*.[49]

Unarmed pike, this is an unpainted pike.

The two types of infantry firearm used in this period were the **caliver** and **musket**, but there was another firearm in service. This was the **bastard musket**, a short-barreled version of the musket sometimes referred to as a caliver; neither the bastard musket nor the caliver used a rest as the musket did.

---

49 Los Tercios en lascampanas del Mediterraneo s.XVI (Italia), Almena, Madrid 2000, Eduardo de Mesa & Emilio Arredondo, pp 12–13, 55.

Appendix I

A Captain's Commission

Captain Scrope's commission comes from Wiltshire and was sent personally to him from the lord lieutenants of the county. It includes the size of the company that he is to command and a warning to do his duty.[1]

Whereas his Majesty's service and the safety of the Kingdom is much concerned with the careful choice of able and sufficient officers, to order and regulate the trained bands of the several counties within his Majesty's Dominions in the best in the best and most approved way of Military Discipline. I have therefore according to his Majesty's trust reposed in me on that behalf and out of a due consideration of the good fame and constant report your sufficiency and willingness for such a service hath deservedly gained you, fixed upon and do by these points make choice of, and appoint you to continue Captain of that company of foot consisting of a hundred which you held in the time of my honoured and deceased brother. And I do farther in my own, require and authorise you, but in his Majesty's name strictly will and command you to the uttermost of your power to see the said company well ordered and disciplined in such sort that upon all occasions it may be fit and ready for his Majesty's service: In the execution and performance whereof you are to proceed according to and be guided by such instructions as from time to time either from myself or the Colonel for the said Regiment shall be given unto you. Whereof you are not to fail at your peril and as you would annoy his Majesty's displeasure. And this is to be your sufficient warrant and discharge. Whitehall this 25th of November 1630.

Pembroke Montgomery

To my loving friend Captain John Scroope

---

1   British Library, Add MS 28212, folio 76

The following example is from Gloucestershire and is dated to 1631, and date-wise can be compared to the very slightly earlier one.[2] Again it is a personal letter to the named captain. It contains instructions, more so than the Wiltshire commission:

Whereas it hath pleased the kings most excellent majesty by his patents under the great seal of England bearing date the 17th day of July in the 6th year of his reign to confer upon me the Lieutenancy of his county of Gloucester and the city of Gloucester and county of the said city and thereby to invest in me the power and authority thereunto belonging. These are therefore by virtue of the said commission to authorise you, Nathaniel Stevens, esquire, from time to time, as often as you shall see sufficient cause, at least twice yearly to assemble, muster and call together to such place or places, as you shall think convenient, all that company of foot heretofore under your conduct and command in the lifetime of my dear father and them carefully to view, train and discipline in martial feats, so as they may be fit for his majesty's service if occasion shall be offered. And if upon the muster and view taken, you shall find any of your number wanting or any defect or insufficiency of persons, arms or munition, you shall not only do your best endeavour as far as in you lyeth, for the due supply speedy reformation and furnishing of the same, and for the careful pursuance thereof hereafter. But you shall as soon as you can conveniently acquaint 2 of the Deputy Lieutenants of this county therewith, that dwell nearest to the place where your company live; to the end that they may assist you in the performance hereof and by these psents I do further authorise you to order and dispose your said company into several squadrons under the inferior officers [your] discretion shall [direct] you requiring you to cause a particular roll or book to be made of all the names of your said company, their armour, weapons, munitions, furniture and other military provision and the same to be returned unto me about the later end of June next, your keeping a true copy thereof for your own use. And if any of your company shall happen to die or else by old age or any other infirmity or disability are or shall be come unfit for service or shall depart this county by special license, you shall address yourself to 2 of the Deputy Lieutenants that dwell nearest to your said company and acquaint them therewith requiring to place and enrol in the stead of such as either shall die or become defective or depart the county as aforesaid, such meet persons as they in their discretions shall think fit, so that your number continue still as many as now they are. And finally I do by these psents authorise you to punish any person or persons, either officers or common soldiers belonging to your band that shall be found disobedient or obstinate defective in the execution of the pmises according to the quality of their offence, and not otherwise, and for your due proceeding in these services and effectual performing of the same these shall be your sufficient warrant given under my hand and seal the 17th day of April in the 7th year of his said majesty's reign of England, Scotland, France and Ireland, AD 1631

2   Gloucestershire Archives, D547a/F6.

Appendix II

An Oath of a Chief Constable

This document comes from Suffolk and is dated to about 1622.[1] The chief constable would have been required to take this oath on his appointment to the post.

> Whereas you are elected to be one of the Chief Constables within the Hundred of ……… in the place of ……….. late Chief Constable there you shall swear that during all such time as you shall continue in the same office you shall without delay, well and truly, to the uttermost of your skill & power execute all manner of precepts, warrants and mandate to you, or your partner Chief Constables of the same hundred, lawfully directed or to be directed and believed & there of shall in due time true return and certificate make without any connivance or partiality whatsoever.

> You shall also keep the peace in your own person & execute the conservation of his Majesty's peace for such as shall lie in your power.

> You shall make search for the suppressing as well of unlawful plays & games as drunkenness & idleness & what you shall find therein you shall duly certify to the end the offender may be punished.

> You shall well and indifferently according to your best understanding tax and proportion every town within your division to such rates as shall be imposed upon your said division either for provision of his Majesty's most honourable household or for any other states and taxations for public service as well the money by you to be received towards the said taxes and rates or any of them as also all other monies as shall come to your hands or which you shall be trusted to take & do receive as one of the Chief Constables of the hundred aforesaid you shall truly & in due time pay without any wilful subtraction.

> You shall do your endeavour duly to keep your petty sessions in such sort as they have usually been heretofore kept within your hundred & there shall likewise

---

1   British Library, Add MS 39245, f.51.

endeavour to find out servants to fit masters for such wages as are or shall be allowed by the statutes & laws of this Kingdom and lastly you shall do & perform all things that belong to the office & place of a Chief Constable so long as you shall therein continue as God shall give you grace, so help you God.

Appendix III

A Drummer's Warrant, 1636

This warrant was given to John Rudd to authorise him to teach drumming to the drummers in the trained bands.[1]

Whereas we have received a petition from our servant John Rudd, declaring unto us the insufficiency of the drummers serving the trained bands in the several counties of this our kingdom, although we have heretofore given special directions by our mediate command for the beating of one kind of March appointed by us whereby the complete English March may be observed as anciently it hath been, we taking the same unto consideration, do therefore hereby authorise the said John Rudd (of whose knowledge & experience we are well satisfied) & such others as he shall appoint to direct & instruct drum beaters in all the trained bands within the several counties of this our kingdom & see them furnished with good drums, and as many drummers to each company as he and his said deputies shall think fit, for that a uniformity may be held in the said Marches. And for his the said John Rudd and his deputies pains & service herein our will & pleasure is, and we do hereby require you to assign him satisfaction yearly, according to your discretions. Given under our signet at our Palace at Westminster the first day of June in the twelfth year of our reign.

---

1   British Library, Harley MS 4014, f.23.

Appendix IV

Captain Ashenhurst's Warrant, Essex

The captain, in this case Captain Ashenhurst, having received his orders from the Lord Lieutenant to muster his soldiers, has in turn, written to the town of Maldon, Essex,[1] with his instructions for the planned muster in 1633.

To the Bailiffs of Maldon

By virtue of warrant from the right honourable Robert Earl of Warwick Lord Lieutenant of this county these are to will & require you to charge the petty constables within your liberties to five warning to all the trained soldiers of the foot company within their limit committed to my leading as well new supplies as others to appear before and completely armed with good & serviceable arms at the Blue Boar in Maldon on Thursday being the seven & the eight day of this instant June by nine of the clock in the forenoon, and that every musketeer bring with him half a pound of powder & match proportionable thereto, to be spent in exercise of their arms, and that the petty constables fail not also to bring with them the Sergeants entertainment, which by the Grand Jury was thought fit for them to have & ready in advance of their service, which is six pence for every arm to be then bought & paid for this year's service with the arrearages for the year past and that every one charged with arms have particular warning that you be ignorant hereof, and that all which be warned for their service be sufficient & able men of person being householders, and that the said petty constables be present themselves at the time and place aforesaid bringing with them true returns fair written of the names of all such as they shall warn for this service hereof I pray not to fail as you respect his Majesty's service. Dated 13 June 1633

Your loving friend

Arthur Ashenhurst

---

1   Essex Record Office, D/B 3/3/406.

Appendix V

Training Manual, Derbyshire

This training manual comes from Derbyshire and is dated to no later than 1624.[1] It is handwritten with a number of hand-drawn diagrams. The original layout has been retained, as has one original diagram with the kind permission of the Derbyshire Record Office. To aid the reader, emphasis is added to subheaders.

To the Right worshipful, Sir Henry Willoughby, knight, Baronett, Justice of the Peace, and (quozi) within this county and one of his Majesty's Deputy Lieutenants for the same.

Right worshipful well weighty and considering your noble and hierarchical mind which you have always borne unto the offices of martial discipline affairs. And your willingness in fostering the same is the cause which makes me so bold to present this small book unto your serious view hoping you will peruse it at your best leisure. And so I rest thereby your worship to be commanded

Geo D

Right worshipful, I might here set down the office of the:

General
Marshal General
The Quarter Master General
The Colonel
The Lieutenant Colonel
The Sergeant Major
The Quarter Master of a Regiment
The Provost of a Regiment

---

1   Derbyshire Record Office, D2375/F/K/1/6/11.

But in regard there is no such officers used amongst our Private and Trained Bands I will omit them and set down only the office of:

The Captain
The Lieutenant
The Ensign
The Sergeant
The Corporal
The Lansprisado
And the Drum, all which officers do belong to a foot company.

The office of a Captain of foot

When he receives his company and his arms; he is to choose his men and to sort them to their arms as he shall think fit, provided that he make his ablest men pikes and his broad men musketeers, he shall choose his officers such as others have had in the like places and are of experience and good government; or such as have made themselves to be fit for the like.

He shall divide his company into three squadrons or corporalships.

He shall take care and see that his soldiers be taught the fine use of their arms, to keep their orders in marching or in battling, to understand all manner [Molyors] and sounds of the drum: In marching with his company he shall be in the head of the company going towards the enemy and in the rear coming from an enemy.

In leading he shall take his quarter assigned according to his degree and place in the regiment and shall see it be to and ordered according to the directions his superior officers have received and that there be divisions both of the quarter into squadrons and the squadrons into comoradoes or fellowships. He shall have his quarter kept sweet for health, fullness and quiet for order especially in the night.

If his whole company be appointed to watch he shall draw out his company and stand in arms ready to march before his after attending the directions of the Sergeant Major of the regiment for placing of his Corpo de Garde setting forth his sentinels and sending out his round and see the directions given him performed. He is not to abandon his Garde till he be relieved and what service is described and brought to that Corpo de Garde where he is. It shall be by him sent to the Captain of the watch, and he shall still make good his garde if he be not commanded by a superior officer to retire.

If he hears of any mutiny or discontented humour tending to mutiny committed by any of his company within his quarter, he shall forthwith advertise his Colonel or if he be not in the way, some public officer of the army and that he attach and bring forth the party offending, with such witnesses and proofs as are to be produced; of which if he fail and know it he shall be held very faulty and if such things escape him he shall be held unworthy of his place.

In matter of service he shall do all that is commanded him by any superior officer that hath authority, in the best sort he can without either exceeding his commission or doing less.

Lastly, when he is alone with his company he shall be very vigilant and careful both in marching and lodging, and if he be put to any extremity yet he might look to make accompte, and therefore he shall do the utmost both by judgement and valour to free his troops.

The office of the Lieutenant

When the company is present he shall be an assistant to his captain in seeing all directions performed that are commanded by a superior office, all such as his captain hath authority to command and in the absence of the captain he shall have the same authority the captain hath.

In marching if there be no company but his own; he shall be at the one end of his company when the captain is at the other end; And if the company march with the regiment, he shall take such place, as the superior officers that have authority shall assign him.

In lodging he shall be placed on the right hand of his captain, as near the end of the quarter as convenient may be and shall in all service and at all times, help to keep the soldiers in discipline and obedience and shall perform all things commanded him, which are necessary to be done by him with valour and [ingenuity].

The office of an Ensign

When his captain or lieutenant are present he shall be assistant unto them or either of them and in their absence have the same authority the captain has.

In marching he is to carry his ensign and take such place as shall be assigned him and if his company be alone he shall either upon entering his quarter, going out of his quarter, going upon his guard or upon the sight of an enemy, carry his ensign advanced and flying, and if he march with a regiment he and all the other ensigns shall do as the ensign Colonel do.

In fight he shall ever carry his ensign advanced and flying without offering to use it in any kind of offence, being the sign for the company to gather by, and therefore to be observed; for which cause for his defence he is to use his sword.

If he march with other ensigns he shall take such place as shall be assigned him. The ensign shall never turn his face out of his order, start from any danger nor forsake his ensign upon pain of death when so ever the drum shall beat for the gathering of the company together, he shall be in the place, and shall see the ensign well guarded and be ready to march or do anything for the service.

The office of the Sergeant

If all the three forename officers be out of the way by any accident, then the eldest sergeant is to command the company as next in place.

In assembling the company he shall set every man in his place and if any be missing he shall look them out, and have power to correct them and if any be defective and not to be found, he is to acquaint his captain or officer with it.

When the company is assembled and set in order, he shall march on the outside where he may best see the order of march observed, and to make the places of sergeants more certain the eldest shall march in the right flank and take care from the ensign forwards and the youngest sergeant on the left flank and take care from the ensign backward.

He is to understand the use of all arms usually carried and all things else that belong to a soldier, yet he is especially to make himself able to direct and lead shot because if his company be alone and have any fight, he is by custom to conduct the shot, in which case he is to follow the directions given him by his captain, or in his captain's absence, any of his superior officers.

And for his more particular directions how to lead his shot after that he hath brought them up to that ground, and in that number and order that his captain or superior officer hath directed him, he shall have every man come up to him and see him take his level and discharge to a good purpose; as also he shall see the shot keep their order as well in going or as retiring, and therefore look to the order of that part on which he is assigned to attend.

The oldest sergeant shall lodge in the strict of the quarter right behind the captain, and the other sergeant in the like sort right behind the lieutenant.

And in the quarter they are both to visit the soldiers' lodgings and to see them orderly and quiet.

He is also to fetch the word from the Sergeant-Major of the Regiment, and deliver it to his captain, lieutenant and ensign and to the corporal that is of the watch, if the whole company watch, he is to attend, and to see the places where the sentinels are put out, and to visit them all, if the watch by squadrons, then he shall lead the squadrons to bring them to their ground, where he shall attend upon any extraordinary occasion by the appointment of the captain of the watch, And whilst he is there he is to advertise the captain of the watch, of any extraordinary discovery or accident of any importance.

He shall deliver such munitions, either of victuals or of war to the corporals of the company, as he shall receive or fetch from the Sergeant-Major of the Regiment.

The office of a Corporal

Though it very seldom happens that he has charge of the company, yet if such an accident should fall out, that all the superior officers were absent then the command belongs to him.

To his place belongs properly, the command of one squadron of the company, which he is to divide into comoradoes or fellowships, to see all that are within that squadron well exercised in their arms, to keep them and wear them soldier like, to deliver munitions of victuals or arms to govern the watch, work or service, and to take care in every respect that they do the duties of good soldiers.

When the drum beats to the gathering of the company, the corporals are to be in readiness themselves, and to call together their squadrons with which they shall repair to their colours, and if any of their squadron be wanting without leave they shall give notice thereof to their captain, and shall execute the said absence to the punishing of them.

He shall have at the least a third part of the company under his squadron which being divided into files he himself shall be leader of the chief file, and with the same always so take place on the right hand of his squadron, which shall be composed of the two sorts of arms now in use: pikes and muskets.

He shall not in case of any default by absence leave the place void and unsupplied, unless the same fall out to be the leader or bringer up, whose places shall ever be supplied by the next.

In marching and fighting, the Corporal of the company hath no command, but of the file which each of them leads: they are to see to the opening of ranks and files, and to the doubling of the same, to follow the sound of the drum and to observe every other motion that shall be commanded by the chief officers, always provided that he start not out of his place, nor use any command of himself.

When his squadron is to watch, he shall at the sound of the drum assemble them and repair to his ensign, and shall see them fully furnished of their arms, powder, match, bullets and all things else that shall be necessary to the arms they carry, whereof they shall be supplied by the Sergeants of the company.

He is to be led by his Sergeant to the place of his watch, and from him to receive the word and directions, in what manner and where he shall place his sentinel, as well by day as by night which he is to see performed.

His sentinel being placed, he is to let none pass his guard without the word, unless the captain of the watch, or the Sergeant-Major.

To whom after he knows them he is to deliver the word the first round only.

In taking the word, he is never to go further forth then the sentinel next the Guard, and when the outermost sentinel gives him warning of the approach of any, he is to make his guard stand to their arms, and to take three or four out among them, and so attend their coming, having given direction to his outmost sentinel for that end, to let them pass, when they are approached near him, he is not to advance out to them but to call out one of the company, if more than one come together to him, and so receive the word from him; when the corporal hath warning of his or their coming he shall draw his sword and set it against the breast of him of whom receives the word within the defence of three soldiers he took with him, who shall have their pikes charged and their matches cocked until such time as the corporal hath received the word and given order to let them pass.

He shall so divide his sentinels that every man's task be alike, he shall see them changed at due times, and shall now and then visit them unlooked for.

He must warn his sentinels not to give false alarms, but with as silent as is possible, to advertise his said corporal, who upon any extraordinary occasion, shall make his squadron stand to their arms, and give notice of the danger discovered to the next guards and to the captain of the watch.

He shall make good the place of his guard, till he be called from there, and not suffer any of his squadron to leave the same till he be relived and he shall fulfil on his guard, all commands that shall be published for the entering or going forth of the soldiers.

At the coming of the relief he shall put his squadron in arms, stand ready to receive them and when his sentinels are relieved march to his quarter.

If during the time of his watch any of his squadron shall have offended he is to commit them and to acquaint his captain and chief officers therewith.

If by any occasion of the company's remove he be drawn from his guard before 24 hours be expired and that the company lodge again within the said time, then shall the said corporal with his said squadron, be in readiness to watch out the residue of the time in such place as he shall be appointed.

Lately as the corporal is next in degree to the sergeant, so in behaving himself well, he may attain to the place of a sergeant when by any accident it shall be void.

The office of a Lanspresadoe

Next to the corporal is the Lanspresadoe who in the absence of the corporal, is in every respect to do his office, his own proper place is to lead the left hand file, of the squadron and to have of his own, and the files adjoining the same care for the observing of their orders, as is specified in the corporals office.

The office of the Drum

There ought to be two drums in a company, and both perfect in every necessary sound hereof, who by tunes are to do all service belonging to the place, And therefore both in field and garrison, one of them is ever to give attendance in the quarters, though the company should at any time be freed of their duty.

The drum having warning to beat to the gathering of the company, shall beat from one end of the quarter to the other, twice and shall repair to his Ensign's lodging.

When the company marches, one of them shall sound by turns and one relieve the other when the company shall be joined with others the drums shall take place by the appointment of the Drum Major, and shall sound the same point, and observe the time that the drum doth that is next to the colonel or chief officer.

It is the office of a drum, when any of the company are taken prisoners, to enquire after them, and to carry their ransom which he may boldly do after he has received a passport from the general or chief commander of army or garrison, where the company is when he is come near to any place of the enemy's he is to sound thrice and not to approach to near, till he be fetched in by some of the enemy. He is only to make his errand known, and not to discover anything of the state of the place where he is sent that in may be prejudicial to it, and to take as much notice as he can of all such things and concern the enemy what his coming back he shall discover to the General or Chief Officer.

It is his duty being in garrison and have the main guard; not to go without leave of the Captain of the watch, and to be there all night to beat and alarums if need require, for which use he must be perfect to practise on his sticks because the enemy shall take no notice thereof; he must beat the relief in the morning after day break and to set the parade.

The company of soldiers is to consist of two sorts, that is; gentlemen and sentinels or common soldiers.

The office and duty of a gentleman is to be always ready when it cometh to his turn to watch, And then he is to go the round; or lie perdue as occasion be, if he lie perdue he is to be brought to the place by a sergeant and if he be laid next to the enemy whether they lie in garrison or in the field, if he discover the enemy to fall out of the town or out of their trenches; he shall not upon pain of death upon every slight occasion to give an alarums, for the disquieting of the Army; But one comes he to fight with him, if two to retire to the next perdue; and the two to combat with them.

Military Directions

And so if he discover three or four still to retire to the next so long as they are able to march before they give any alarum. If they be to go the round they are to take directions from the Captain of the watch or such an officer as he shall appoint to command them.

The duties of sentinel or common soldier is to be ready at the sound of the drum and to be at the command of his corporal and to stand sentinel and do all other things he shall be commanded by his corporal being needful and expedient.

Therefore he that desires to be a soldier of an assured quality, to the end he may be able to persevere in each enterprise, and bear out every brunt stoutly and serve sufficiently, he ought have a strong body, sound and free from sickness and of a good complexion, so shall he be able to resist the continual toil and travel which he of necessity must daily take, a continual and extreme cold in the winter inordinate heat in the summer, in marching in the day keeping sentinel in the night, and in cold cabins, in secret ambushes,

And likewise, in trenches, where perhaps he shall stand many hours, in the waters, snow, or mire up to the knees, and besides upon bulwarks, breaches, inspyalls, sentinel perdue and such like, when occasion requires and necessity constrains of all which exploits and discommodity he must be a partaker.

Wherefore that man that is not of such sufficiency in body to the end he may not spend his time in vain, it is very requisite that he resolve himself to exercise some other profession for though some do hold and opinion that few men be strong by nature, but many be exercise and industry, yet not withstanding thought of body is to be required, in respect that a soldier must be as well acquainted, and as able to bear continual travel; yea and to put on a resolute mind, to endure all the miseries and hazards of warlike affairs.

He with means to attain and attribute to himself the honourable name of a soldier, must first employ his time in practise of those arms wherewith he intends to use; to apply his time, that when any enterprise shall call him forth to make proof thereof, he may be able to handle his pike or musket with due dexterity and assured agility since those both weapons wherewith now Mars do arms his warlike troops and tries each doubtful fight of bloody battle.

It is necessary that in the exercising of your motions, you exercise the whole company together as follows;

These are the general words of command which are to be used;

Stand right in your ranks

Stand right in your files

Order your pikes

Silence

To the right hand

By facing to the right hand, you bring your ranks into files and your files into ranks and in standing in that order, you make the front and rearward the naked flanks of your battle.

The right wing the forward and the left wing the rear.

This is to be done when the enemy give a charge or encounter on the right side overthewarte your battle; as the service of the horsemen is most commonly commanded in that order.

For the Rutters [Reiters] will never if they can otherwise avoid it, give an assault or onset at the face of the shot, therefore they always wheel with a career about at the left advantage enforcing to break your array.

This order of facing is also very requisite to draw of and give time to your seconders and relievers a fresh to charge the enemy

And sometimes you shall find it needful and convenient to gain the benefit of the ground; or otherwise to draw your men out of the danger of the enemy artillery.

As you were;

To the left hand.

In facing to the left hand all things are to be observed as is noted in facing to the right.

As you were;

To the right hand about.

By facing about to the right hand you make your front the rear and the rear the front. This is most commonly done in bringing of your men to retire.

Sometimes it will be needful to face back to the right hand to answer the charge of the enemy at the rearward which happens often in service upon a sudden.

As you were;

To the left hand about

By facing to the left hand about you must observe all things as in facing to the right had about.

As you were;

To the right hand round about.

This is to be done when you perceive the enemy doth intend to take a view of your forces

For by that means they shall be disappointed of their purpose, and especially if it be done with naked swords in their hands which will be an occasion not only to blind them, but also will strike a sudden terror in them.

It is likewise necessary to face and wheel about being prepared to receive the violent charge of the enemy.

As you were;

To the left had round about.

This facing round about to the left hand is to be done as is laid down in the facing round about on the right had.

As you were;

Ranks to the right had double.

As you were;

The doubling of ranks to the right hand is both needful and necessary to be done when you perceive the enemy goes about to discover the number of your ranks then and to command half your men to step forward and so to double your ranks and in so doing it will appear unto the enemy that you are stronger than indeed you are and besides the Cornet discover your number by reason of the thick ranks, for then you lie open on both sides, yet can they not learn anything by the forward.

Moreover if you be commanded to attend with your men within the danger of the artillery shot being planted overthwarte the flank of your battle, then having doubled your ranks you stand not in half the danger as otherwise should by reason of drawing up half your men and lying open on both sides which is an occasion that they shall will play betwixt the galleries without any great loss of your men.

As you were.

Ranks to the left hand double.

In doubling your ranks on the left hand it is to be observed and followed in all points as is prescribed in doubling the ranks on the right hand.

As you were.

Files to the right hand double.

Likewise as I have touched afore it is a good course to double your files for the eschewing of the enemy's force shot of ordnance, being politically planted before the front of the battle, for in so doing the shot will pass through the open galleries from the forward to the rearward and so throughout without any great harm except it happen by some mere chance.

And also if they be to march through a straight passage by doubling their files they may easier march without confusion.

As you were.

Files to the left hand double.

In doubling your files to the left hand, you are to do in every point, as set down in doubling the files to the right hand.

As you were.

Middle men in the right hand double your front.

This doubling of the front is sometimes serviceable for that your men take less room at the rearward than in doubling of the ranks for having 20 ranks of men you lead 10 ranks of them from the rear, and having ten you lead up five ranks, And it is contrary when you double your ranks middlemen.

As you were.

Middlemen to the left hand double your front.

In doubling of the fronts on the left hand they are to advance pikes from the middle rank downward and so to march up and double the front.

Middle men as you were.

Bringers up to the right hand double your front.

Bringers up, as you were.

Bringers up to the left hand, double your front.

Bringers up, as you were.

To the right hand countermarch.

To the left hand countermarch either so often as you please.

Having these exercised your motions the whole company together you are to draw out your pikes a good distance and exercise them as follows;

Musketeers to your rendezvous

Standing postures belonging to the pike.

Stand right in your ranks

Stand right in your files

Silence

Order your pikes

Advance your pikes

Order your pikes

Shoulder your pikes

To the front charge

Shoulder as you were

To the right hand charge

Shoulder as you were

To the left hand charge

Shoulder as you were

To the rear charge

Shoulder as you were

Port your pike

Shoulder as you were

Trail your pike

Check your pike

Recover and charge to the front

Advance your pike

Trail your pike with the boot and forward

To the rear charge your pike

Shoulder your pike

Order your pike

Advance your pike

Lay down your pike

These following postures are to be done either marching or standing

March

To the front charge

Shoulder as you were

To the right hand charge

Shoulder as you were

To the left hand charge

Shoulder as you were

To the rear charge

Shoulder as you were

To the right and left hand charge by division

Shoulder as you were

To the front and rear charge by division

Shoulder as you were

Port your pikes

Trail your pikes

Recover and charge to the front

Shoulder your pikes

Trail your pikes with the boot and forward

To the rear charge

Shoulder your pikes

Order your pikes

Advance your pikes

Lay down your pikes

Pikes to your rendezvous

These following postures belong to the musketeers standing.

Musketeers handle your arms

Take up your musket

Join your musket and your rest

[Peace] your musket

Shoulder your musket

Slip your musket

Unshoulder your musket

Rest your musket

Balance your musket

Finger your match

Blow your match of your pan

Cock your match

Try your match

Blow your match and guard your pan

Present

Give fire

Uncock your match

Put again between your fingers

Close your pan

Prime your pan

Close your pan

Cast off your loose corns

Cast about your musket and trail your rest

Open your chargers

Charge your musket

Draw out your scourer

Shorten your scouring stick

Take your bullet out of your mouth

Ram in your bullet

Draw out your scouring stick

Shorten your scourer

Return your scourer

Recover your musket

Recover your rest

Shoulder your musket

These following postures belong to the musket marching.

March

Slip your musket

Unshoulder your musket

Join your musket and rest

Finger your match

Blow match of your pan

Cock your match

Try your match

Blow your match and guard your pan

Present

Give fire

Dismount your musket

Join your musket and your rest

Uncock your match

Put it between your fingers

Close your pan

Prime your pan

Cast off your loose corns

Cast about your musket and trail your rest

Open your charges

Charge your musket

Draw out your scourer

Shorten your scourer

Take your bullet out of your mouth

Ram in your bullet

Draw out your scouring stick

Return your scourer

Recover your musket

Recover your rest

Shoulder your musket

After you have these exercised your shot and pikes apart you shall join them together in one battalia as follows;

Shot	Pikes	Shot
S SSSSS	O OOOOOOO	S SSSSS
S SSSSS	O OOOOOOO	S SSSSS
S SSSSS	O OOOOOOO	S SSSSS
S SSSSS	O OOOOOOO	S SSSSS
S SSSSS	O OOOOOOO	S SSSSS
S SSSSS	O OOOOOOO	S SSSSS
S SSSSS	O OOOOOOO	S SSSSS
S SSSSS	O OOOOOOO	S SSSSS
S SSSSS	O OOOOOOO	S SSSSS
S SSSSS	O OOOOOOO	S SSSSS

A Battle consisting of four score pikes and six score shot.

A square of men in their ranks		The ranks doubled

1 O OOOOOOOOO 1 O
OOOOOOOOOOOOOOOOOOOO

2 O OOOOOOOOO 2

3 O OOOOOOOOO 3 O
OOOOOOOOOOOOOOOOOOOO

4 O OOOOOOOOO 4

5 O OOOOOOOOO 5 O
OOOOOOOOOOOOOOOOOOOO

6 O OOOOOOOOO 6

7 O OOOOOOOOO 7 O
OOOOOOOOOOOOOOOOOOOO

8 O OOOOOOOOO 8

9 O OOOOOOOOO 9 O
OOOOOOOOOOOOOOOOOOOO

10 O OOOOOOOOO 10

Here you may plainly see the manner of the doubling of ranks for whereas you were ten deep in the first place your ranks being doubled you are but five deep as may appear.

A square of men   **Front ranks**

```
O OOOOOOOOO        O     O     O     O     O
                         O     O     O     O
O
O OOOOOOOOO        O     O     O     O     O
F
                         O     O     O     O
O      i
O OOOOOOOOO        O     O     O     O     O
l
                         O     O     O     O
O      e
O OOOOOOOOO        O     O     O     O     O
s
                         O     O     O     O
O
O OOOOOOOOO        O     O     O     O     O
d
                         O     O     O     O
O      o
O OOOOOOOOO        O     O     O     O     O
u
                         O     O     O     O
O      b
O OOOOOOOOO        O     O     O     O     O
l
                         O     O     O     O
O      e
O OOOOOOOOO        O     O     O     O     O
d
                         O     O     O     O
O
O OOOOOOOOO        O     O     O     O     O
                         O     O     O     O
O
O OOOOOOOOO        O     O     O     O     O
                         O     O     O     O
O
```

Here you may plainly see the manner of the doubling of files, for whereas you were but ten deep in the first place you are twenty deep, your files being doubled as may appear.

The Manner of a single cross battle

	Pikes	
Pikes	Short weapons & ensigns	Pikes
	Pikes	

A Battle called Spinola's Cross

Shot	Pikes	Shot
Pikes	Short weapons & ensigns	Pikes
Shot	Pikes	Shot

The Manner of a Battle with two Battles of Succour

Battle

Rearward

The Manner of framing five Battalias, two of them being Battalias of succour

	2	3
Battalia	Battalia	Battalia

2

Battalia   Battalia

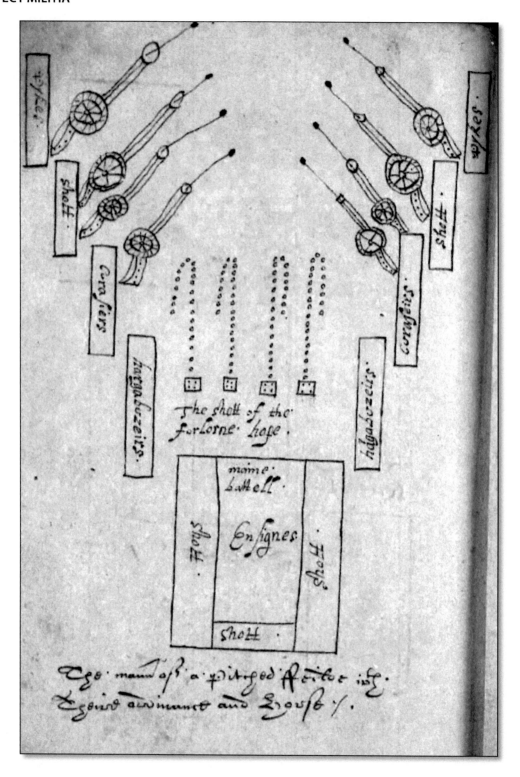

The Manner of a pitched filed with their ordnance and horse. (Reproduced with the kind permission of Derbyshire Record Office)

Appendix VI

Training Manual, Hampshire

This manual comes from Hampshire and is undated but is contemporary with the period being studied[1]. It is had written and includes a large amount of very interesting information on conduct in the field making it more of a field manual rather than a training manual.

The Exercising of a foot Company

For to do the Revolutions there are five distances to be observed.

The first is when everyone is distant from his fellows six foot square that is in file and rank.

And because the measures of such distances cannot be taken so instantly by eye, the distance of six foot between the files is measured when the soldiers stretching their arms do touch one another's hands, and between the ranks when the end of their pikes come well nigh to the heels of them that march before, And the measure of three foot between the files is when the elbows touch one another's, and between the ranks when they come to touch the ends of one another's rapiers.

For to march in the field the distance of three foot from file to file is kept, and of six foot from rank to rank.

For to order themselves in battaill as for to go towards the enemy the distance of three foot in file and rank is observed, and likewise in conversion and wheeling.

The musketeers also going to shoot by rank kept the same distance of three foot, going to skirmish do go a [ladis] band which is out of order.

There is yet another sort of distance which is not used but for to receive the enemy with a firm stand and serves for the pikes only. For the musketeers

1   Hampshire Records Office, 44M69/G5/48/1.

cannot be so closed in files because they must have their arms at liberty. And that is when everyone is distant from file to file a foot and a half and of three foot from rank to rank and this last distance is this commanded; Close yourselves (thoroughly). But his Excellency will not have the last distance should be taught to the soldiers, but when that necessity shall require it.

They will close themselves very much upon their own accord without command.

To begin therefore to do the exercises the company being set to the first distance, to wit of six foot in file and ranks then this is said.

But before you begin to exercise you must draw up all your musketeers on the right hand of your pikes. Then each officer takes out one musketeer out of a file to see him do over all his postures first going then standing and so all the rest, till each musketeer have done them all, or so many as be used full. That being done then order your ranks and files to there just distance of six foot, the chief officer must go along the front and right flank to see if the soldiers stand right as he hath commanded them. Then this is said.

"Stand right in your files and ranks." These words of command are often to be used in excel.

"Silence"

"To the right hand: As you were:"

"To the left hand: As you were:"

"To the right hand about: As you were:"

"To the left hand about: As you were:"

In turning either to their right hand or left hand they must remove their pikes.

You must note that when they are commanded to go, "as they were", they must return from where they departed; as if they double to the right hand they must return to the left, and so contrary.

The chief officer that doth exercise must after every motion, go along the front and right flank, to see if ranks and files be in their right order and distance, to amend them but not to go among the ranks and files: Then to return to the front to give the next command.

"Ranks to the right hand double: Ranks as you were:"

"Ranks to the left hand double: Ranks as you were:"

There must be care had that they double (always) in the middle of the space of six foot, that they may stand in all three foot in their files.

"Files to the right hand double: Files as you were:"

"Files to the left hand double: Files as you were:"

They must turn always to the right hand when the half files do return to their places.

"Half files to the right hand double your ranks: Half files as you were:"

"Half files to the left hand double your ranks: Half files as you were:"

In countermarching they are new bid to advance their pike but they are to that of themselves, and also in setting them down they must always put a little forward, that foot which is answerable to the hand they turn on, to turn upon it, and the rest of the rank to come up to the places from whence the first rank did move.

"Files to the right hand countermarch:"

"Files to the left hand countermarch:"

To the right or left hand at discretion;

The chief officer that doth exercise the company must lead the files and ranks through when they do countermarch a fast pace and to stand where the last rank stood before.

"Ranks to the right hand countermarch:"

"Ranks to the left hand countermarch:"

"To the right or left hand, as you were."

"To the right or left hand, countermarch and lose ground."

When you will wheel to the right hand, double your ranks to the left hand, and when you will wheel to the left hand, double your ranks to the right hand, for so the right and left hand leaders will keep their places on that corner which you wheel.

"Ranks to the left hand double:"

You must close from both the outsides to the middle and so likewise to both the outsides from the middle to open and to stand in their distances of three foot in their files. This closing your files is to be used in a double company.

"Close your files."

"Close your ranks."

"Upon three foot distance and no more."

When there is no hand named, the middlemost file must not stir, the next file on both sides keep to the rest of the files, to the right and left hand until they are all gone to their places, this when the ranks are not doubled and serve for a double company:

The outmost man that is in the corner that you wheel, he must keep his pike ordered on the ground and the outermost musketeer when you wheel to him, his rest must remain fast in his hand on the ground, the soldiers must have an eye to him that stands still in the corner, not to break from him but to keep on three foot from another. An officer must always lead the corner about sometimes to stand at a quarter of the circle and sometimes half and three parts of the (road), as the officer shall see occasion

Or convenient, they must do it in the rear, as they have done it in the front.

"To the right hand wheel:"

"To the left hand wheel."

"Rank open backward to your double distance."

"In your double distance to wit at twelve foot and this is for single company."

"Rank as you were."

"Open your files to wit at first distance of six foot."

When there is no hand named, the next files to the middlemost files on both sides keep close to the rear of the files to the right and left hand till they are gone six foot from the middle file, and then stand still if you be gone to face he comes closer up to the middle file to take his new distance, and see all the rest of the files one after another.

The pikes are taken apart from the musketeers and one officer doth exercise them in their standing postures till the chief officer hath exercised the musketeers in discharging by rank.

For the pikes with a firm stand.

1. Advance your pike
2. Order your pike
3. Shoulder your pike

4. Slope your pike
5. Order your pike
6. Trail your pike
7. Check your pike
8. Charge your pike
9. Shoulder your pike

They must likewise observe in charging, standing to fall back with the right leg.

"To the right hand charge, shoulder your pikes."

"To the left hand charge, shoulder your pikes."

"To the rear charge, shoulder your pikes."

"Order your pikes."

The following motions are to be performed marching.

"Advance your pikes and march."

When the troops stir, the last rank, must move as soon as the first rank.

"Charge your pike, shoulder your pike."

"To the right hand charge: Shoulder your pike."

"To the left hand charge: Shoulder your pike."

In marching they must always step forward with the left leg and foot but in charging to the right or left hand they must step back with the right leg and stand a while till the officer doth bid them march.

"Charge to the rear; shoulder your pikes."

"Trail your pikes; order your pikes and stand."

The pikes in charging must be no closer in files and rank than three foot, marching they must go but a reasonable space to keep their ranks in order, and when they are bid to charge to do it leisurely till they have brought up their left foot before and then having their pike must march up a reasonable (void) pace toward the enemy till the officer see other things.

In charging to the right or left hand they fall back with the right leg and stand a while till the officer bid them march.

For the musketeers there are but three words of command to be used to them which are these following;

"Make ready."

"Present."

"Give fire."

Here is to be noted that if a company be of 200 heads; that then the musketeers must be divided into two divisions or streets of six foot to be between each troop for the rank to fall through to turn to the right hand, for a troop of musketeers must never be above the number of pikes at highest.

Also musketeers must observe in all their motions to turn to the right hand and that they have their pieces so high the (noch) be carried (even) with his girdle bearing it two inches from your body and also when they hold their pieces guarded to come to give fire.

In advancing towards the enemy when they do skirmish in troops they must give fire by two ranks or one as it shall be found fitter. The chief officer of the troop commands two ranks to make ready, which are to march forward a reasonable pace doing his postures till he be ready, which will (be) done in ten or twelve paces going with the chief officer that leads up the ranks seeing them ready doth cause the first rank to present or give fire, they levelling at the girdle of a man, the second rank (use) their rests within half a foot of his leader's right foot that his body may be six foot from the rank before with his musket and rest and guarding his own being shut and as soon as the foremost rank hath shot the uttermost man of the right hand must fall away apace from before his fellows that the rest may follow him to give them freedom they going one after the other in file along close by the right hand file of the musketeers, the others through the spaces of six foot till they do come in the rear to fall into their right places, where every man must follow his own file. The second rank must present and shoot to follow after them in all points the second officer being at the head of the troop of the musketeers to lead them safely on then send up more ranks to the chief officer also as the second rank have shot, doing all things as the foremost ranks have done.

To note that when the first rank doth move from the troop the second rank doth follow in six foot distance of the first rank.

Another manner there is to give fire returning from an enemy which is forward after this sort.

As the troop marchs from the enemy the hindermost rank of all keeps with his troop still and walks ready which the officer seeing them ready commands them to present then the soldiers all in that rank (and) all together blowing their matches and then round upon their right legs and then present upon the left leg and so giving fire marching presently a round pace to the front in a file where every man is to fall in his right file by turning themselves round to the right hand as soon as the first rank turns to give fire, the next that make ready and doth as the former and so to the rest.

We give fire by the flank thus, the outermost file next the enemy must be commanded to make ready keeping still along with the body till such as they be ready. Then the officer that commands the file to present to the right of left hand according to the sight of the enemy, either upon the right or left flank, and give fire together when they have discharged, not to stir but to keep their muskets upon their rests toward the enemy and to prime their pans standing and then turn coming up with the right leg, now as soon as the foresaid file doth turn to give fire, the uttermost next that makes ready always keeping along with their troop ever in their rank till the bringer up be past a little beyond the leader of the file that gave fire last and then the whole file must turn only with the right leg before and give fire and do in all points as the first did, and so all the rest one after another. A sergeant must stand at the head of the first file and as soon as the file hath given fire he is to lead forward the first file up to the second that shot and so to the rear one after another till he hath gathered up the whole wing.

Last of all the troops of musketeers, make ready all together their muskets being rested and every soldier to guard the pan being shut (up), the officer, commands the first rank to give fire without advancing from the places where they stand and speedily to fall from before the front of the troop that the rest may the sooner give fire at the doing the same sufficiently one after another this must be done more speedily than any other way of shooting.

His Excellency will not have that any pace or poles should belong to the musketeers but their own pales which God hath given them but to be newly taught the motion or handling of their arms they serve with.

For the shooting at a mark there must be a halberd set up where the soldiers must begin their postures and another halberd some twenty paces off, and the mark some two hundred and twenty or 200 and 50 paces off. Every soldier when he hath shot must fall in the rear of his own file.

There must be always commandment given to the musketeers that they have always small dry priming powder.

To command them also that they lock their matches long enough for else the weight of the match behind holds that the lock will not come home in the pan.

A measure charge must be given to every soldier that holds just as much powder as half the bullet weight at ten to the pound to fit his charge of the bandoleer.

A double company of 200 heads march half of the shot before the pikes and the other half behind for a single company all the musketeers do march before the pikes the first rank of musketeers must march in six foot of the officer that leads.

The officer that leads the pikes must march in six foot of the last rank of musketeers, and the first rank of pikes must keep in six foot of the officer who leads them.

The drums must accommodate themselves in the space that is behind the third rank and before the fourth rank which is six foot.

Orders commanded by his Excellency to be observed in marching as followeth;

In marching the drum beats shall always march and beat between the third and fourth rank both of pike and musketeers at the first stroke of the drum the ranks in the rear shall be as ready to stir and march as those of the front for the avoiding of ruin or more hasty marching, than they do in the front.

The distance between each rank in marching shall be six foot from each other so that the heads of the pike may almost touch the heels of the leaders.

The files shall be but three foot from each other.

When the regiment marchs by divisions the half of the musketeers shall march before the pikes in the middle and the other half of the musketeers after. Observing that at last they march no less than ten in depth because the ways are commonly there unto, keeping the distances both of rank and files aforesaid.

The officers that lead any division of the regiment, shall take no more place for himself than the distance of one rank, which is six foot to the end that one may follow another the better and neither time nor place left in marching, And that officer that marches after and division of the regiment shall follow the last rank of them that marches before at the distance of six foot so that between him and that officer which leads any following division of that regiment shall be but six foot which makes the distance between both the divisions to be eighteen foot.

Now if the regiment be divided into two troops or divisions then that second division of the regiment shall follow the other at the distance of ten or twelve strides and no wider.

The distances between the regiments that march one after another shall be 18 or twenty strides, that is six foot before the officer that brings up the rear of the regiment before, and six foot allowed for the officer aforesaid.

Between the tercios of the army the order of distances shall be kept that is about twenty or 25 strides having a special care that the rear be not too far behind, to the end no time nor place may be lost in marching.

And when the breadth of the ground shall permit then shall the regiment march in one body, observing the distance both of ranks and files as aforesaid.

When the regiment marches in one body then shall the pikes march before the musketeers after the pikes leaving a distance between the body of the pikes & the body of the musketeers of fifty foot.

Between every five files at the most and between every five files at the least of the musketeers shall be a street of six foot breadth keeping as much as is possible the musketeers of each company together which musketeers also as far forth as may be, shall be placed right against the pikes of that company.

The regiment standing in battallie if it be divided into two divisions the one division shall stand fifty foot from the other. And if the musketeers be more in number than the pikes and so consequently are (bigger) than the body of the pike, then they draw themselves inward after the body of the pike that stand before them.

As in this (manner).

But in case the number of musketeers be too great and that both in regard of the streets of six foot distance which are made between them as also in regard of their number there be no place enough to draw them all without touching one another, then shall both the troops of musketeers draw out unto both the field alike of the pikes that stand before them.

Thus

All the women and boys of the regiment shall march after their respective regiments, none of them shall be suffered to march neither above or at the sides of the regiment, the care and charge thereof shall laid upon the Provost Marshal of that regiment.

You must make your ranks at double distance or twelve foot causing them to make ready. Then if you will have them to give fire to the right hand you must cause the right hand file to stand still and the rest of the rank to march all together to the right hand into that file which stands still. Then you may make them present and give fire. The same order when you will do it to the left hand.

Memoranda when they have given fire they must fall back into their ranks.

To give fire by introduction

You must cause them all to make ready the first rank only giving fire which done the second rank advances through and beyond the first rank six foot presents and give fire which done the 3rd rank advances through and beyond the second rank present and give fire and subsequently the rest.

When you (are) not disbanded do it thus.

From your wing of shot draw out one file fifty paces making ready as you march when you are within distance of the enemy cause your file presently to fall with two ranks, when the first hath presented and given fire he falls away and so doth the second marching into the wing again, in file as he first come out;

You must have a care that the second file be ready to present and give fire as the fist did so soon as it is fallen off; thus you may maintain fight longer with most ease.

A rule agreed upon at (the) leaguer by all the Colonels of the places of marching in division to the end we should all observed our manner who were of our nation

1. The first place is the front or head of the pikes.

2. The second place is the rear of the pikes who command all, the rear being drawn up in battalia.

3. The third place the leading of the right wing of shot.

4. The 4th place the leading of the left wing of shot.

5. The fifth place in the rear of all which if that place (fale out) for a lieutenant to command them he is (?? ??) at the capt divisions that commands the rear of the pikes as often changing as the capt shall please. But if a capt command the rear of all then he is not to change place.

6. The sixth place is the leading of the second division of pikes.

7. The seventh is the leading of the third division of pikes.

8. The eighth place, the leading of the fourth division of pikes and if there be more officers that want places as lieutenants (??) let him march with his own capt somewhat after because the leading of pikes is held more honourable than shot.

The next places are the bringers-up of the divisions of pikes, and if there be more officers that want places as lieutenants then tell him march with his own capt somewhat after.

The sergeants are to be commanded upon both sides of the flanks of the divisions to keep their men in rank and file orderly, the sergeants not being permitted at any time to lead a division without express command.

For the colours they are either to march in the head of a company or division towards an enemy and from an enemy in the rear, but in sight in the fourth or fifth rank.

Also the musketeers are always, both in division and single company, to march before the pikes when they go to their guard and so face about when they come from their guard holding every man his place.

As leading a company to the guard the capt marches before the musketeers, the colours in the head of the pike, the lieutenant in the rear so coming off a guard the lieutenant leading the pike, the colours in the rear of pikes, the capt in the rear of all.

Degrees of places to be observed when the Companies join, in division.

First, the companies to join according to the capt's antiquity, the elder on the right hand;

1. The first place, the vanguard of pike.

2. Rear of all the division marches out by division then he that commands the rear of all is to march in the rear of all. But when the division is in battalia then he is to march in the rear of the pikes about the middle and to see the whole rear be in order.

3. Leading the right wing of shot.

4. Leading the left wing of shot.

5. Rear of pike

6. .The pikes being divided, leading the half of the pikes as if there be four sub-divisions, the leading of the third sub-division.

7. Rear of right wing of musketeers

8. Rear of left wing of musketeers.

9. Second sub-division of the right wing of shot.

10. Second sub-division of the left wing of shot.

If the troop be so great as there be many sub-divisions and many lieutenants to place them the eldest to be placed in the leading of the first sub-division of pike that hath no leader appointed. The second, in the first sub-division of musketeers of the right wing that hath no leader, the third in the first sub-division of the left wing that hath no leader; Now if the troop be grown so little and the officers many as there be few sub-divisions and no distinct places for everyone, the capts being placed and the sub-divisions furnished with leaders & bringers up, the remaining lieutenants to lead with their captains or to be disposed in what other places he that commands the division shall think fit.

Those that command the musketeers must observe that always when the troop draws into battalia that they put their wings of shot into sub-divisions as when their files are at three foot distance the sub-divisions must be at six foot and when their files be at six foot distance their sub-divisions at twelve foot:

Note that when you will exercise the Battalion in their motions you must never put them into sub-divisions but when you exercise your musketeers in (??) you must of necessity do it, and the sub-divisions at twelve foot.

Note that you must never make your sub-divisions of musketeers of above five files or less than three.

The colours are to march between the third and fourth ranks of pike.

The sergeants to bring up the rear of sub-divisions and those which remain to be placed on the flanks of the pikes, and musketeers the eldest capt; the third rank to the front, the second in the seventh rank, so as one be upon one flank of the division and the other upon the other.

You must observe to place more sergeants with the musketeers than with the pikes.

The drums, when you march in sub-division to beat between the third and fourth ranks but when you march in battalia to place them in the flanks so towards the front, the other towards the rear.

If the Colonel, Lieutenant-Colonel and Sergeant-Major be absent then the elder Capt to have no set place but to dispose of those places as if he were an officer of the field, and himself to be free to be in any place where there shall be use of him.

The officers when they bring their companies to join and have any odd men they shall bring them to the head of the troop in a file so as the next company joins their odd men together; and they must observe that he which hath more odd men, the other must join to him to make up his file.

They must never put their odd men into a rank but into a file for an odd rank brings disorder in the Battalion which a file doth not.

Finis

Appendix VII

The Deputy Lieutenants of Yorkshire

Yorkshire was the largest county and had the largest trained band, 12,000 foot and 400 horse. Needless to say, they also had the largest number of deputy lieutenants. The following list makes no claim for completeness, and undoubtedly there should be more names on it; the present author is not aware of any comprehensive lists of deputy lieutenants prior to the Civil War. The sources are listed as footnotes.

The Lord Lieutenant was given authority to appoint his own deputies in 1608.

Sir William Alford of Meaux Abbey and Bilton in Holderness, elected as an MP in 1625, 1626 and 1628, he was serving as a deputy lieutenant of the East Riding by 1623 and continued until at least 1629 and again from at least 1635 to 1642 when he probably died.[1]

The Archbishop of York, on 21 August 1615, was placed in charge of the trained band of the city of York by the Privy Council.[2]

Henry Belasyse of Oulston, elected as an MP six times between 1625 and 1644, served briefly as a deputy lieutenant for the North Riding in 1642, initially opposing the King, but sat as an MP in the Oxford Parliament; his brother was the governor of Newark in 1646.[3]

George Boteler or Butler of Ellerton, elected twice to Parliament, 1614 and 1621, he was serving as a deputy lieutenant of the East Riding by 1633–38 and continued until at least 1639. He was also the captain of the East Riding's

---

1 <http://www.historyofparliamentonline.org/volume/1604-1629/member/alford-sir-william-1571-1642> accessed 12 February 2017.

2 Dasent, *Acts of the Privy Council of England*, 1617–1619 pp.362–3.

3 <http://www.historyofparliamentonline.org/volume/1604-1629/member/belasyse-henry-1604-1647>, accessed 13 February 2017.

horse troop prior to the Civil War.[4] He lived in York during the Civil War but gave only passive support to the King.[5]

Sir Matthew Boynton of Barmston was elected as an MP in 1621 and again after the Civil War. He was appointed by Wentworth to serve as a deputy lieutenant, he served for the East Riding from 1629 to 1638, and was also in the trained band as the colonel of a foot regiment from at least December 1625 to 1638. He lost his post due to his moving out of the county. He returned in 1641 and fought for Parliament in the Civil War, and died in 1647.[6]

Sir Hugh Cholmley of Whitby was elected as an MP five times between 1624 and 1640, he was a deputy lieutenant of the North Riding of Yorkshire 1636–40 and was also a colonel in the trained band, 1636–40.[7] In May 1642 he was nominated by Parliament as a commissioner to negotiate with the King. He says in his memoirs that Pym ordered him to summon the trained bands to oppose the King but he refused on the grounds that this would start a war and so Pym backed down.[8] In the Civil War he initially sided with Parliament but changed sides in 1643.

Sir Phillip Constable of Everingham, noted as a deputy lieutenant for the East Riding in 1613, he died in 1619.[9]

Sir William Constable of Flamborough, elected to Parliament four times between 1626 and 1642. In 1613 he was appointed as captain of a trained band company in the Dickering Wapentake in the East Riding, and was a colonel from 1629–37. He served intermittently as a JP from 1613 until his death in 1655, and was appointed as a deputy lieutenant by Wentworth, serving for the East Riding of Yorkshire from 1629 to 1637; a friend of Sir Matthew Boynton. Sir William left the country but returned in 1641. During the Civil War he fought for Parliament, raising his own regiment, and was a regicide, he died in 1655.[10]

Sir Thomas Danbye, selected as sheriff in 1637 and noted serving as a deputy lieutenant for the North Riding from 1633–35 until at least 1639.[11]

---

4   British Library, Add MS 28082, f.81.
5   <http://www.historyofparliamentonline.org/volume/1604-1629/member/boteler-george-1583-1657>, accessed 14 February 2017. Also Historical Manuscripts Commission, *The Manuscripts of the Earl Cowper*, pp.205, 208.
6   <http://www.historyofparliamentonline.org/volume/1604-1629/member/boynton-sir-matthew-1592-1647>, accessed 14 February 2017
7   <http://www.historyofparliamentonline.org/volume/1604-1629/member/cholmley-hugh-1600-1657>, accessed 30 January 2017.
8   Jack Binns, *The Memoirs and Memorials of Sir Hugh Cholmley of Whitby, 1600–57*, p.103.
9   British Library, Add Ch 66608.
10 <http://www.historyofparliamentonline.org/volume/1604-1629/member/constable-sir-william-1591-1655>, accessed 17 February 2017.
11 West Yorkshire Archives Service, 32D86/38, f.258; British Library, Add MS 28082, f. 81; Historical Manuscripts Commission, *The Manuscripts of the Earl Cowper*, vol. II, p.208.

Sir Thomas Fairfax I of Denton and Nun Appleton, 1st Baron Cameron, he was elected to Parliament five times between 1586 and 1625, and served as a deputy lieutenant for the West Riding from at least 1614 to at least 1639; he also served in the trained band foot of the West Riding from 1587 until his death in 1640, rising from captain to colonel with service in the Low Countries and Cadiz.[12]

Sir Thomas Fairfax II of Walton and Gilling Castle, elected as an MP five times between 1601 and 1626, noted as a deputy lieutenant for the North Riding in 1633. He was a captain in the trained band by 1599 and a colonel by about 1635. Created Viscount Fairfax in 1629, he died in 1636.[13] Being a trained band officer meant that he had more than a passing interest in the 1626 bill brought in to regulate the position of the county muster masters.

Sir Thomas Finch, served as a Justice of the Peace for the East Riding from 1618 to at least 1636. Sir Thomas was a native of Kent, so why he was in Yorkshire is not understood.[14] He also served as a deputy lieutenant in the East Riding in 1625, when he attended the musters, he died 1634.[15]

Sir John Gibson of Welburn, elected as an MP in 1621 and selected as sheriff in 1630, he was serving as a deputy lieutenant by 1633 and served until his death in 1639, he also served as a captain of horse in the trained band in the North Riding. His son fought for the Royalists in the Civil War.[16]

Sir Henry Goodricke of Ribston Hall, a deputy lieutenant for the West Riding by 1633–35 and until at least 1639.[17] He died in 1642 aged 62 and is buried at Little Ribston near Harrogate.

Sir Henry Griffith, 1st Baronet of Burton Agnes, noted as a deputy lieutenant in 1613,[18] he died in 1620. He was the father of Sir Henry Griffith, 2nd Baronet.

Sir Henry Griffith, 2nd Baronet, of Burton Agnes, he was a deputy lieutenant for the East Riding in 1636[19] and served until at least 1639.[20] He was the eldest

12 <http://www.historyofparliamentonline.org/volume/1604-1629/member/fairfax-sir-thomas-i-155960-1640>, accessed 21 February 2017.

13 <http://www.historyofparliamentonline.org/volume/1604-1629/member/fairfax-sir-thomas-ii-1576-1636>, accessed 15 October 2019.

14 <http://www.historyofparliamentonline.org/volume/1604-1629/member/finch-sir-thomas-1578-1639>, accessed 2 June 2017.

15 Thomas Sheppard et al. (eds), *The transactions of the East Riding Antiquarian Society*, vol. 21 (Hull: A. Brown and Sons, 1915).

16 <http://www.historyofparliamentonline.org/volume/1604-1629/member/gibson-sir-john-1576-1639>, accessed 23 February 2017.

17 West Yorkshire Archives Service, 32D86/38, f.258; British Library, Add MS 28082, ff.80–81; Historical Manuscripts Commission, *The Manuscripts of the Earl Cowper*, Vol. II, p.208.

18 British Library, Add Ch 66608.

19 Christopher Watson (transcr.), *A Muster Roll of the East Riding of Yorkshire (1636)* (Chorley: C.J. Watson, 2002).

20 West Yorkshire Archives Service, 32D86/38, f.258; Historical Manuscripts Commission, *The Manuscripts of the Earl Cowper*, Vol. II, p.208.

son of Sir Henry Griffith, 1st Baronet, and his sister married Sir Mathew Boynton, another deputy lieutenant. He was colonel of a trained band foot regiment in 1639. He sided with the King during the Civil War and fought at Marston Moor. He died in 1654 aged 51 and is buried in Burton Agnes.

Sir Christopher Hildyard of Winestead, elected to Parliament 10 times between 1589 and 1628, he was serving as a deputy lieutenant for the East Riding by 1613 and continued to serve until his death in 1634.[21]

Sir Thomas Hoby of Hackness, elected to Parliament 10 times between 1589 and 1628, he served as a deputy lieutenant for the North Riding from 1623 until 1637, he was a staunch puritan and a difficult man to deal with, he was removed from the deputy lieutenancy due to his disagreements with Sir John Hotham and Sir Hugh Cholmley. He was also the colonel of a trained band foot regiment in the North Riding; he was probably removed from the colonelcy of this regiment in 1636 and replaced by Sir Hugh Cholmley. He died in 1640.[22]

Sir John Hotham, of Scarborough, elected to Parliament five times between 1625 and 1640, he was one of the deputy lieutenants for the East Riding of Yorkshire in 1625 and again in 1629–40; he was also a colonel in the trained band, 1635–43.[23] Sir John sided with Parliament at the start of the war, refusing King Charles access to the arsenal at Hull, in 1643 he tried to change sides but was arrested and executed for treason by Parliament in 1645.

Sir Arthur Ingram, junior, of Temple Newsam and York, he was elected as an MP nine times between 1609 and 1640. One of the major landowners in Yorkshire, died in 1642.[24] He was selected as sheriff in 1629 and was serving as a deputy lieutenant for the West Riding by 1633–35 until at least 1639.[25]

Sir William Lister, a deputy lieutenant for the West Riding by 1633–35 and continued until at least 1639.[26] He died in 1650 and was buried in Thornton near Bradford.

William Mallory, Esq., a deputy lieutenant for the West Riding in 1638 and 1639.[27]

21 <http://www.historyofparliamentonline.org/volume/1604-1629/member/hildyard-sir-christopher-1568-1634>, accessed 24 February 2017.

22 <http://www.historyofparliamentonline.org/volume/1604-1629/member/hoby-sir-thomas-1566-1640>, accessed 24 February 2017.

23 <http://www.historyofparliamentonline.org/volume/1604-1629/member/hotham-sir-john-1589-1645>, accessed 30 January 2017.

24 <http://www.historyofparliamentonline.org/volume/1604-1629/member/ingram-arthur-1565-1642>, accessed 9 January 2019.

25 West Yorkshire Archives Service, 32D86/38, f.258; British Library, Add MS 28082, ff.80–81; Historical Manuscripts Commission, *The Manuscripts of the Earl Cowper*, Vol. II, p.208.

26 West Yorkshire Archives Service, 32D86/38, f.258; British Library, Add MS 28082, ff.80–81; Historical Manuscripts Commission, *The Manuscripts of the Earl Cowper*, Vol. II, p.208.

27 West Yorkshire Archives Service, 32D86/38, f.258; Historical Manuscripts Commission, *The Manuscripts of the Earl Cowper*, Vol. II, p.208.

Sir Thomas Mettam, serving as a deputy lieutenant for the East Riding from at least 1625 until at least 1639,[28] he raised a regiment of foot for the King in the Civil War and was killed at Marston Moor in 1644.[29] He was also the colonel of a trained band foot regiment at the time of the 1st Bishops' War.

Sir Edward Osborne, Baronet, of Kiveton, he was elected as an MP in 1628, and twice in 1640, by 1635 he was serving as a deputy lieutenant for the West Riding. By 1633–35, until at least 1639, he served as a captain in the trained band horse in the West Riding and was lieutenant colonel of Yorkshire's trained band horse. On the outbreak of the Civil War he joined the King and fought with the cavalry.[30]

James Pennyman, Esq., of Ormesby and Marske, noted as a deputy lieutenant in 1633–35.[31] He sided with the King in the Civil War.

Sir William Pennyman of Marske Hall, selected as a sheriff in 1635, he was a deputy lieutenant for the North Riding in 1638 and 1639,[32] and the colonel of a trained band regiment by 1639.

Sir John Ramsden of Byram Hall, selected as sheriff in 1636 and noted as a deputy lieutenant for the West Riding in 1638 and 1639.[33]

Robert Rockley, Esq., of Worsbrough, a Justice of the Peace and also a deputy lieutenant for the West Riding in 1638 and 1639.[34]

Sir Edward Rodes of Great Houghton, a deputy lieutenant for the West Riding in 1638 and 1639.[35] Between 1633 and 1635 he was in command of a trained band foot regiment comprised of 1,000 men raised in the wapentakes of Strafforth, Tickhill, Osgoldcross and Staincross.[36] He sided with Parliament in the Civil War.

Sir William Savile of Thornhill, a deputy lieutenant for the West Riding in 1638 and 1639.[37] He was the colonel of a trained band foot regiment between at least 1633–35 and 1639. He fought for the King in the Civil War and was

28   West Yorkshire Archives Service, 32D86/38, f.258; Historical Manuscripts Commission, *The Manuscripts of the Earl Cowper*, Vol. II, p.208.

29   Thomas Sheppard et al. (eds), *The transactions of the East Riding Antiquarian Society*.

30   <http://www.historyofparliamentonline.org/volume/1604-1629/member/osborne-sir-edward-1596-1647> accessed 1 March 2017.

31   British Library, Add MS 28082, ff.80–81.

32   West Yorkshire Archives Service, 32D86/38, f.258; Historical Manuscripts Commission, *The Manuscripts of the Earl Cowper*, Vol. II, p.208.

33   West Yorkshire Archives Service, 32D86/38, f.258; Historical Manuscripts Commission, *The Manuscripts of the Earl Cowper*, Vol. II, p.208.

34   West Yorkshire Archives Service, 32D86/38, f.258; British Library, Add MS 40132, ff.43–45; Historical Manuscripts Commission, *The Manuscripts of the Earl Cowper*, Vol. II, p.208.

35   West Yorkshire Archives Service, 32D86/38, f.258; British Library, Add MS 40132, ff.43–45.

36   British Library, Add MS 28082, ff.80–81.

37   West Yorkshire Archives Service, 32D86/38, f.258.

near York in 1644.

Sir William Sheffield of Mowthorpe, Terrington, he was elected as an MP twice, in 1614 and in 1624, by 1635 he was serving as a captain in a foot company of the North Riding trained band. He also served as a deputy lieutenant from 1638 to 1642. Despite having Parliamentarian sympathies he decided to leave the country when the Civil War began and so moved to Holland where he died in 1646.[38]

Sir Edward Stanhope, a deputy lieutenant for the West Riding by 1633–35,[39] and continued until at least 1638.[40]

Robert Strickland of Brafferton was elected as an MP twice, in 1624 and 1640, in 1640 he became a deputy lieutenant, holding the post until the outbreak of the Civil War. Before this, in 1638, he had become a colonel in a trained band foot regiment in the North Riding. In the Civil War he fought as a Royalist.[41]

Christopher Wandesford, Master of the Rolls in Ireland and a deputy lieutenant for the North Riding in 1638.[42]

Sir George Wentworth of Woolley, noted as a deputy lieutenant for the West Riding in 1638 and 1639,[43] and the colonel of a trained band foot regiment in the same year.

38 <http://www.historyofparliamentonline.org/volume/1604-1629/member/sheffield-william-158990-1646>, accessed 13 March 2017.
39 British Library, Add MS 28082, f.81.
40 West Yorkshire Archives Service, 32D86/38, f.258.
41 <http://www.historyofparliamentonline.org/volume/1604-1629/member/strickland-robert-1600-1671>, accessed 13 March 2017; British Library, Add MS 36913, f.45.
42 West Yorkshire Archives Service, 32D86/38, f.258.
43 West Yorkshire Archives Service, 32D86/38, folio 258& The Manuscripts of the Earl Cowper, Vol. II, HMSO, London, 1888, p208

Appendix VIII

The Oaths of Allegiance and Supremacy

These oaths took various forms during the reigns of James and Charles. These versions are dated to 1642 and are as originally printed.

The Oath of Supremacy

I *A. B.* do utterly testifie and declare in my Conscience, that the Kings Highnesse is the onely Supreame Governour of this Realme, and all other his Highnesse Dominions and Countries, as well in all Spirituall or Ecclesiasticall things or causes, as Temporall: And that no forraine Prince, Person, Prelate, State or Potentate, hath or ought to have any Jurisdiction, Power, Superiorities, Preeminence or Authority Ecclesiasticall or Spirituall within this Realme. And therefore, I do utterly renounce and forsake all Jurisdictions, Powers, Superiorities, or Authorities; and do promise that from henchforth I shall beare faith and true Allegiance to the Kings Highnesse, his Heires and lawfull Successors: and to my power shall assist and defend all Jurisdictions, Priviledges, Preheminences and Authorities granted or belonging to the Kings Highnesse, his Heires and Successors or united and annexed to the Imperial Crowne of the Realme: so helpe me God: and by the Contents of this Booke.

The Oath of Allegiance

I A. B. doe truely and sincercly acknowledge, professe, testifie and declare in my conscience before God and the world, That our Soveraigne Lord King CHARLES, is lawfull King of this Realme, and of all other His Majesties Dominions and Countreyes: And that the *Pope* neither of himselfe, nor by any Authority of the Church or Sea of *Rome,* or by an othermeanes with any other, hath any power or Authority to depose the king, or to dispose of any of his Majesties Kingdomes or Dominions, or to Authorize any Forraigne Prince, to invade or annoy Him or His Countreyes, or to discharge any of his Subjects of their Allegiance and Obedience to His Majestie, or to give Licence or leave to any of them to beare Armes, raise Tumults, or to offer any violence or hurt to His Majesties Royall person, State or Government, or to any of His Majesties Subjects within His Majesties Dominions. Also I doe sweare from my heart, that, notwithstanding any Declaration or Sentence of Excommunication or Deprivation made or granted, or to be made or granted, by the *Pope* or his Successors, or by any Authority derived, or pretended to be derived from him or his Sea, against the said King, His Heires or Successors, or any Absolution of the said Subjects from their Obedience; I will bear faith and true allegiance to His Majestie, His Heires and Successors, and Him and Them will defend to the uttermost of my power, against all Conspiracies and Attempts whatsoever, which shall be made against His or their Persons, their Crowne and Dignitie, by reason or colour of any such Sentence, or Declaration or otherwise, and will doe my best endevour to disclose and make known unto his Majesty, His Heires and Successors, all Treasons and Traitorous Conspiracies which I shall know or heare of to be against Him, or any of them. And l do further sweare, That I do from my heart abhor, detest and abjure as impious and Hereticall this damnable Doctrine and Position, That Princes which be Excommunicated or deprived by the *Pope*, may be Deposed or Murthered by their Subjects, or any other whatsoever. And I doe beleeve, and in conscience am resolved, that neither the *Pope*, nor any person whatsoever hath power to absolve me of this Oath, or any part thereof; which I acknowledge by good and full Authority to bee lawfully ministered unto me, and do renounce all Pardons and Dispensations to the contrary. And all these things I doe plainely and sincerely acknowledge and sweare, according to these expresse words by me spoken, and according to the plaine and common sence and understanding of the same words, without any Equivocation, or mentall evasion or secret reservasion whatsoever. And I doe make this Recognition and acknowledgement heartily, willingly, and truely, upon the true Faith of a Christian. So helpe me GOD.

Cleare your Pann

4

Bring up your Musket with the left hand only, towards your mouth and blow your pan stifly not stooping vpon any termes and in the meane time with your right hand take your touch box as in the figure

Appendix IX

Fairies and Devils

This letter, although dated, and having names and places included, could not with any confidence be placed in any particular county or associated with a known person. The letter came from the Bodleian Library and was in the Tanner MSS.[1] It is included here simply because the participants were all armed as soldiers, presumably equipped as the trained band soldiers would have been.

> This I coppied out of a ltr from my brother Ashton to my brother Tatton dated February the 16th 1638.
>
> Our schoolmaster brother who teacheth schoole at Ashly neere Harwood, in a ltr brought hither this day writes for a truth, his owne eyes being witnes that at a hill called Stansnostleiffe in Knasbury Forrest their dayly appeares many fairies, Satyres or divells traineing wth pikes & muskets, with Bandaleers about their necks, wch many thereabouts have seene. To wch report I give so much credit, the same in effect being related by others, that my young cozon Key & I were att the chardge to send Mr Thargot thither to morrow to see & learne the truth thereof soe hereafter you shall heare more.
>
> Thus far my Brother Aston
>
> This I had from Mr Rich: Brereton of Ashley

---

1   Bodleian Library, Tanner MSS 67, f.54.

Bibliography

Atkinson, E.G. (ed.), *Acts of the Privy Council of England*, Volume 34, 1615–1616 (Nendeln/ Lichtenstein: Kraus-Thomson Organization Ltd, 1974)

Barnes, Mike, *Hampshire Militia Muster Rolls*, Numbers 1–31 (Moreton-in-Marsh: privately published, n.d.)

Barnes, Thomas Garden, *Somerset 1625–1640: A County's Government During the "Personal Rule"* (London: Oxford University Press, 1961)

Barriffe, William, *Military Discipline: or, the Young Artilleryman* (London: 1635)

Bearman, Robert, (ed.), *Minutes and Accounts of the Stratford upon Avon Corporation*, Volume VI, 1599–1609 (Stratford-upon-Avon: The Dugdale Society, 2011)

Binns, Jack (ed.), *The Memoirs and Memorials of Sir Hugh Cholmley of Whitby, 1600–57* (Woodbridge: Yorkshire Archaeological Society, 2000)

Bourgeois II, E.J. (ed.), *A Cambridgeshire Lieutenancy Letterbook, 1595–1605* (Cambridge: Cambridgeshire Record Society, vol. 12, 1997)

Bond, Shelagh (ed.), *The Chamber Order Book of Worcester, 1602–50*, WHS volume 8 (Worcester: Worcestershire Historical Society, 1974)

Boynton, Lindsay, *The Elizabethan Militia: 1558–1638* (London: Routledge & Keegan Paul Ltd, 1967)

Clark, Peter, Alan Smith, Nicholas Tyacke (eds), *The English Commonwealth 1547–1640*, Chapter 5, 'Militia Rates and Militia Statutes, 1558–1663', A Hassell-Smith (Leicester: Leicester University Press, 1979)

Cogswell, Thomas, *Home Divisions: Aristocracy, the State and Provincial Conflict* (Manchester: Manchester University Press, 1998)

Cooke, Edward, *The character of warre, or The image of martiall discipline* (London: 1626)

Copnall, H. Hampton and Henry B. Saxton, *Nottinghamshire County Records. Notes & extracts from the Nottinghamshire county records of the 17th century* (Nottingham: H.B. Saxton, 1915)

Cottrill, Mrs E. (ed.), *Sir Henry Whithed's Letter Book*, Volume 1, 1601–1614 (Winchester: Hampshire Record Office, 1976)

Dasent, John R. (ed.), *Acts of the Privy Council of England*, Volume 33, 1613–1614 (Nendeln/ Lichtenstein: Kraus-Thomson Organization Ltd, 1974)

Dasent, John R. (ed.), *Acts of the Privy Council of England*, Volume 36, 1617–1619 (London: HMSO, 1933; reprint Nendeln/Lichtenstein: Kraus-Thomson Organization Ltd, 1974)

Dasent, John R. (ed.), *Acts of the Privy Council of England*, Volume 39, 1623–1625 (London: HMSO, 1933)

Dasent, John R., *Acts of the Privy Council of England*, Volume 45, 1629 May–1630 May (London, HMSO, 1960)

Dasent, John R., *Acts of the Privy Council of England*, Volume 46, 1630–1631 (London: HMSO, 1964)

De Gheyn, Jacob, *Instructions for musters and Armes, and the use thereof* (London: 1631)

De Mesa, Eduardo, and Emilio Arredondo, *Los Tercios en lascampanas del Mediterraneo s.XVI* (Italia), Almena, Madrid 2000

J.P. Earwaker, *The Constables' Accounts of the Manor of Manchester from the year 1612 to the year 1647*, Vol. 1 (Manchester: Cornish, 1892)

Earwaker, J.O. (ed.), *The Constables Accounts of the Manor of Manchester*, Volume II, 1633–1647 (n.p., British Library Historical Collection, 2011)

Emberton, Wilfrid, *Skippon's Brave Boys: the origins, development and Civil War service of the London trained Bands* (London: Barracuda Books Ltd, 1984)

Evans, D., *Equipping a C17th Army: an estimate of the English forces required for the War in the Palatinate* (Powys: March Publications, 1985(?))

Fletcher, Anthony, *Sussex 1600–1660: A County Community in Peace and War* (London: Longman, 1975)

Fox, E.T., *Military Archery in the Seventeenth Century: Three Seventeenth-century Texts*, (n.p.: Lulu. com, 2015)

Godwin, Rev G.N., *The Civil War in Hampshire (1642–45) and the Story of Basing House* (Southampton: 1904, revised edition)

Goring, Jeremy, and Joan Wake (eds), *Northamptonshire Lieutenancy Papers and Other Documents, 1580–1614* (Gateshead: Northamptonshire Record Society, Volume XXVII, 1975)

Green, Mary Anne Everett (ed.), *Calendar of State Papers, Domestic Series, of the Reign of James I, 1603–10* (London: Longman, Brown, Green, Longmans, & Roberts, 1857)

Green, Mary Anne Everett (ed,), *Calendar of State Papers, Domestic Series, of the Reign of James I. 1611–1618* (London: 1858; Liechtenstein: Kraus Reprint Ltd, 1967)

Gregory, Ivon L. (ed.), *The Hartland Church Accounts 1597–1706* (Frome: Butler & Tanner, 1950)

Groombridge, Margaret (ed.), *Calendar of Chester City Council Minutes 1603–42* (n.p.: Taylor & Co Ltd, 1956)

Hamilton, Charles S., Ph.D (ed.), *The 'Muster Master', by Gervase Markham*, Camden Miscellany Volume XXVI (London: Royal Historical Society, 1975)

Harland, John, *The Lancashire Lieutenancy under the Tudors and Stuarts*, Volume 2 (Manchester: The Chetham Society, 1859; reprint Forgotten Books)

Hassell-Smith, A., 'Militia rates and militia statutes, 1558–1663', in *The English Commonwealth 1547–1640, Essays in Politics and Society* (Leicester: Leicester University, 1979)

Hinds, Allen B. (ed.), *Calendar of State Papers and Manuscripts, Relating to English Affairs, Existing in the Archives and Collections of Venice*, Vol. XVII, 1621–1623 (London: The Hereford Times Limited, 1911)

Historical Manuscripts Commission, *Tenth report of the Royal Commission on Historical Manuscripts* (London: Eyre & Spottiswoode, 1885)

Historical Manuscripts Commission, *Twelfth Report, Appendix, Part I, The Manuscripts of the Earl Cowper, K.G.* (London: Eyre & Spottiswoode, 1888)

Hobson, M.G. and Rev H.E. Salter, *Oxford Council Acts 1626–1665* (Oxford: Oxford Historical Society, 1933)

Holland, Rev. William, *Cratfield, a transcript of the accounts of the parish from 1490 to 1642, with notes* (London: Jarrold and Sons, 1895)

Jones, S.F. (ed.), *English Army Lists of the Early 1640s* (Reading: Tyger's Head Books, 2015)

Latimer, John, *The Annals of Bristol in the seventeenth century* (Bristol: William George's Sons, 1887)

Livock, D.M., *City chamberlains' accounts in the sixteenth and seventeenth centuries* (Bristol: Bristol Record Society, 1966)

Long, W.H. (ed.), *The Oglander Memoirs Extracts from the mss. of Sir J. Oglander, kt.* (London: Reeves & Turner 1888; reprint Forgotten Books, n.d.)

Lyle, J.V. (ed.), *Acts of the Privy Council of England*, Volume 37, 1619–1621 (London: HMSO, 1930)

Lyle, J.V. (ed.), *Acts of the Privy Council of England*, Volume 40, 1625–1626 (London: HMSO, 1934)

Lyle, J.V. *Acts of the Privy Council of England*, Volume 41, January–August 1627 (London: HMSO, 1938)

Lyle, J.V., *Acts of the Privy Council of England*, Volume 42, 1627 September–1628 June (London: HMSO, 1940)

Markham, Gervase, *The Souldiers Exercise in three books* (London: 1643; reprinted by Partizan Press, 2013)

Monger, R.F. (ed.), *Acts of the Privy Council of England*, Volume 44, 1628 July–1629 April (London: HMSO, 1958)

Morgan, Victor, Elizabeth Rutledge, Barry Taylor (eds), *The Papers of Nathaniel Bacon of Stiffkey*, Vol. V, 1603–07 (Norwich: Norfolk Record Society, 2010)

Murphy, W.P.D. (ed.), *The Earl of Hertford's Lieutenancy Papers 1603–1612* (Devizes: Wiltshire Record Society, Volume XXIII, 1969)

Nottingham, Corporation of, *Records of the Borough of Nottingham*, Vol. 4 (London: Bernard Quaritch, 1884)

Nottingham, Corporation of, *Records of the Borough of Nottingham*, Vol. 5 (London: Bernard Quaritch, 1900)

Overall, H.C. and W.H. Overall, *Analytical index to the series of records known as the Remembrancia: preserved among the archives of the City of London, A.D. 1579–1664* (London: E.J. Francis, 1878)

Parker, Geoffrey, *The Army of Flanders and the Spanish Road, 1567–1659* (Cambridge: Cambridge University Press, 1972)

Pixton, Paul B. (ed.), *Wrenbury Wills and Inventories 1542–1661* (Chester: The Record Society of Lancashire and Cheshire, 2009)

Quintrell, B.W., *The Maynard Lieutenancy Book, 1608–1639*, parts 1 & 2, Essex Historical Documents 3 (Chelmsford: Essex Record Office, 1993)

Rye, Walter, *State Papers Relating to Musters, Beacons, Ship-Money, & etc, In Norfolk, from 1626 chiefly to the beginning of the Civil War* (n.p.: Forgotten Books, 2015)

Salter, Rev. H.E., *Oxford Council Acts 1583–1626* (Oxford: Oxford Historical Society, 1928)

Schofield, Bertram (ed.), *The Knyvett Letters, 1620–1644* (Bishop's Stortford: Norfolk Record Society, 1949), Volume XX

Sheppard, Thomas et al. (eds), *The transactions of the East Riding Antiquarian Society*, vol. 21 (Hull: A. Brown and Sons, 1915)

Slater, Victor L., *Noble Government: the Stuart Lord Lieutenancy and the Transformation of English Politics* (Athens, Ga: University of Georgia Press, 1994)

Smith, John, *Men & Armour for Gloucestershire in 1608* (Gloucester: Alan Sutton Publishing Ltd, 1980)

Stocks, Helen, *Records of the Borough of Leicester, 1603–88* (Cambridge: Cambridge University Press, 1923)

Stocks, J.E., *Market Harborough Parish Records 1531–1837* (London: Oxford University Press, 1926)

Wake, Joan (ed.), *A Copy of Papers Relating to Musters, Beacons, Subsidies etc, in the County of Northampton, AD 1586–1623*, vol. III (Kettering: Northamptonshire Record Society, 1926)

Wake, Joan, (ed.), *The Montagu Musters Book, 1602–1623* (Peterborough: Northamptonshire Record Society, Volume VII, 1935)

Watson, Christopher J. (transcr.), *A Muster Roll of the East Riding of Yorkshire (1636)* (Chorley: C.J. Watson, 2002)

Sir Richard Worsley, *The History of the Isle of Wight* (London: 1781; reprint 1975, E.P. Publishing Ltd)

The many manuscripts consulted have been noted in the relevant chapters and appendices.